JUNGLE BOOK

JUNGLE BOOK

Thailand's politics, moral panic,
and plunder, 1996–2008

CHANG NOI

SILKWORM BOOKS

ISBN: 978-974-9511-63-3

Published in 2009 by
Silkworm Books
6 Sukkasem Road, T. Suthep
Chiang Mai 50200, Thailand
info@silkwormbooks.com
http://www.silkwormbooks.com

Typeset by Silk Type in Garamond Premier Pro 11 pt.
Cover image: Henri Rousseau, Tiger in Tropical Storm (Surprise!), 1891. Reproduced with the permission of National Gallery, London, UK.

Printed in Thailand by O.S. Printing House, Bangkok

5 4 3 2 1

CONTENTS

INTRODUCTION

Chang Noi first padded onto *The Nation*'s editorial pages in April 1996. This book has a selection from almost four hundred articles that have appeared over the twelve years since.

Many, many thanks to *The Nation* for being such a good host. In those twelve years, the paper has not deliberately censored a single word—even though several suits have been launched or threatened by rather important people, and even though Chang Noi's opinions were sometimes at odds with the paper's editorial line. Special thanks are due to Pana Janviroj and Suthichai Yoon, and also to Steven Gan, Jim Eckardt, Thana Poopat, Jeerawat na Thalang, others on the editorial staff, and many people who have offered feedback, encouragement, and criticism.

Thanks also to Trasvin Jittidecharak, Susan Offner, and all at Silkworm Books for their professionalism and friendship.

The articles appear here with only minimal changes. A few sentences have been rewritten for greater clarity, but never with any change of meaning. In some cases the original headline has been used, and in others the improved version invented by *The Nation*'s editors. In one instance, a final sentence has been borrowed from another Chang Noi article. The whole text has been reedited using Silkworm Books' conventions. None of these changes modify the arguments.

Writing this column has been a lot of fun. The twelve years span the bubble, the bust, the fight over the 1997 Constitution, the rise of Thaksin, and the coup and crisis of 2006–8. These years have also seen some big but scarcely noticed changes in the society and its view of itself. Chang Noi has usually tried to avoid the terrain covered by *The Nation*'s editorial team, preferring instead to traipse off into the deep jungles of history, nose into the undergrowth of academia, or simply stomp up a hill in search of a longer, clearer view of the landscape. In this selection, the articles have been grouped to bring out some of the big themes of change over these dozen years.

Fauna is a short handbook on the changing population of the political jungle, focusing on the slow decline of the old godfathers, and the arrival of some new species. *Feeding habits* is about the political food chain and how it has changed with the population.

Water and trees contains several battle stories from the contest over the natural environment. *Culture and custom* tries to capture some of the big over-arching changes in society, and the society's reflection on itself. *Birds, bees, and beasts* is mainly about changing attitudes over sex and gender.

Tooth and claw looks at the weapons used to threaten and destroy basic rights and freedoms, and at some of the heroics in their defense. Finally, *Lords of the jungle* looks at the animals that have been trampling the elephant grass in the last few years.

The top and tail pieces are personal favorites. The first was written for the one hundredth appearance of the Chang Noi column. Although on one level firmly trunk-in-cheek, it's also a serious reflection on how popular feelings are expressed using shared symbols in the public sphere.

The tail piece sums up perfectly how Thai public life over this period makes the observer uncertain whether to laugh or cry, to rage or shrug, to dream or despair—hence the column.

Top piece

THE ELEPHANT AND THE CRISIS

22 June 1999

In Thailand, the elephant is a sacred beast in a very special way. It figures in the religious culture—in the Buddha's birth story, as the Hindu god Ganesh, and in many Jataka tales. It is central to royal history as military equipment, parade transport, and as the magical protector of the realm, the white elephant. But the elephant is much more than a religious and royal icon. It is sacred in a very popular way. Elephants are loved for their unique combination of power and vulnerability. In a curious way, the nation's experience of the crisis has been transferred onto the popular national symbol of the elephant.

To begin with, this has simply been a matter of prominence. Since the crisis hit, elephants have been in the news a lot. There has been a glossy coffee-table book about elephants, at least three art exhibitions on elephant themes, another exhibition of art *by* elephants (the inspiration of a Russian pop-artist), and a documentary film. The prime minister's wife in late 1997 went everywhere clutching a pink elephant doll rigged out in a wedding dress and diamond necklace. Mahidol University announced plans to clone elephants. And of course the mascot for the Bangkok Asian Games was inevitably an elephant.

But the elephant has also conveyed important messages. While nobody had much success in predicting the crisis, close observers of elephants in mid-1997 should have twigged that something was amiss. In the month before the baht floated and sank, an elephant ran amok and hurt a young boy in Samut Prakan; another killed his own mahout in Phayao; two were possibly poisoned by pineapple-growers in Prachuap; and another was rammed by a car in Rangsit. Things were going wrong.

We know now that the worst impact of the crisis came in early 1998. The economy shrank 12 percent with amazing speed. Over 2 million lost their jobs. The numbers in severe poverty shot up by a fifth. The public reaction to all of this was deceptively quiet. No major riots. No mass demonstrations. No noisy public diatribes. No disastrous violence. Of course, in the background there was a gradual and terrible disintegration. More drugs. More gunmen. More violence inside families. More petty crime. More summary killings. But this huge social hurt was somehow disguised. The nation transferred its sense of injury onto elephants. There were lots of news stories about elephants in trouble.

In February 1998, mahouts seized fourteen which were being maltreated by tour operators in Mae Rim. In March, two elephants were killed and burned by pineapple-planters in Kanchanaburi. Another fell off a cliff in the forest divided by the Yadana pipeline. In May, a baby elephant in Surin died from eating pesticide-laced grass. Another adult died from possible starvation. Another was shot in the leg by a poacher. And yet another was badly injured falling down a hill. In October, at least six died in Chiang Mai in disputes between rival tour operators. Another was rammed by a car in Chon Buri. In early 1999, one elephant was wounded by a poacher in Chachoengsao, and a pregnant one was killed by a train in Kanchanaburi.

The epicenter of the crisis was Bangkok, and through mid-year, the press focused on the plight of elephants in the city. Like everyone else, the elephants suffered from unemployment. Like everyone else, they were forced to make a living in desperate and risky ways—tramping the city streets. They were hit by cars and trucks. They were harassed by officials. They stumbled fatally into canals, potholes, and sewers. They fell sick from Bangkok's pollution. The prominent cases were followed night-by-night on the TV news.

Towards year-end, this theme was used as the plot for a whisky ad. A young Adonis drinking in a bar for the rich and beautiful is suddenly drawn to the plight of an elephant mother and child in the crush of night-time traffic. He rushes out and hands over not just all his money, but also his Rolex watch, one of the iconic symbols of affluence in the boom years.

Perhaps it was significant that two of the elephants killed in falls into Bangkok's subterranean infrastructure were called Phang Thong Kham (gold) and Phlai Setthi (millionaire). The elephant had come to represent not just the shock of unemployment, but the collapse of dreams of wealth, the fall of the god of money.

The elephant also became the clearest focus of national feeling. In early 1998, reports trickled in about six Thai elephants which had gone to work in Indonesia. One had already died. The others were being mistreated. They were increasingly at risk as Indonesia's crisis worsened. As months passed, the story became darker. The Thai mahouts had been tricked, short-changed, and packed off home. The deal had been set up by shady middlemen and "politicians." The story took on the shape of tales from the world of human trafficking—initial promises of wealth giving way to trickery, exploitation, and slavery.

A campaign was launched to bring these "Thai" elephants home. Groups got up petitions. The Prime Minister's Office, Commerce Ministry, Forestry Department, and Foreign Ministry were dragged in. International law was invoked. The Indonesians refused to negotiate. Emotions rose. Street demonstrations demanded that the Thai government do something. Activists threatened to bring eighty tuskers into the city to storm Government House to enforce their demand.

This was almost certainly the major threat of public disorder throughout the entire period of the crisis. The call to "bring the Thai elephants home" evoked more nationalist sentiment than all of the protests against the IMF, "selling the country," and the bankruptcy bills. When the five elephants were finally shipped to Phuket, they were welcomed by the governor, the local MP, and a flag-waving crowd who garlanded them as returning heroes. In this crisis, nationalism has been rather half-hearted. But elephantism has been strong.

Elephants also predicted the timing of recovery from crisis. The Thai government and IMF had been forecasting recovery "within six months" since the crisis began, and had long since lost any credibility. But elephants were another matter. Towards year-end, the stories of elephant sorrow dwindled away. In retrospect, we can see this was the time the stock market perked up, exports bottomed, and production indices turned north. Again the clearest message came in an ad, this time for a beer. An elephant is coming through the gate of the ancient city of Ayutthaya—the ancient capital whose destruction in 1767 was evoked many times in comparison to the current crisis. Unlike in the earlier whisky ad, the elephant is not oppressed and threatened. Rather, he is upbeat and resurgent. He is clad in finery, bathed in sunlight, surrounded by traditional dancers, trunk aloft, and preceded by Ad Carabao singing a jubilant anthem and prancing in obvious triumph. Witnessing this display of national resurgence are groups of Japanese and *farang*, who smile and raise their glasses in gestures of restored international confidence from East and West.

If you had read this message of imminent recovery correctly on the first day it appeared, and put your entire fortune on the Thai stock market, you would be over 50 percent richer by today.

Fauna

TWILIGHT OF THE GODFATHERS?

8 June 1996

Is the ugly death of Chaisiri Ruangkanchanaset[1] just another in a long line of grisly endings for Thailand's provincial godfathers? Or does it foretell the end of an era in provincial politics?

The godfathers first rose to prominence a quarter of a century ago. They were made by rising provincial prosperity, coupled with weak or non-existent law enforcement.

The godfathers made money from a heady cocktail of legal, semi-legal, and plainly criminal business. At one end they had crop dealerships, petrol pumps, transport companies, gravel quarries, and all the other types of mainstream business in the provincial towns. At the other they ran underground lotteries, casinos, smuggling rings, and sex businesses. In the middle they had ventures which were technically legal but which generated much larger profits if operated with greater flair—like land speculation, whisky distribution, hotels, government contracting, and logging.

Thailand's military rulers of that era contributed to the rise of the godfather. The military strongmen liked to cultivate powerful friends in the provinces and cared little where these friends got their money. The godfathers in turn decorated their houses with pictures of themselves hobnobbing with their powerful military contacts. These icons served as warning to policemen or other small fry who might have

---

1. Chaisiri Ruangkanchanaset was a long-time MP for Ubon Ratchathani and minister in the governments of Kukrit Pramoj (1975–6) and Prem Tinsulanonda (1983–6). He was believed to run the underground lottery in Ubon and other businesses. He had survived several assassination attempts. On 2 June 1996, a man entered Chaisiri's bedroom and slashed his throat with a machete. The police immediately identified Chaisiri's son Nirandon as the probable mastermind and began a manhunt. Two days later, Nirandon committed suicide. The police believed Nirandon had ordered the murder after a dispute over inheritance.

ideas about challenging the way they did business. "I was a poor man before and did not have much education," explained one of the most successful godfathers of all, "so whatever I do I have to rely on friends and connections in politics."

The godfathers created a gangsterish milieu. They patronized gangs of friends to run their businesses. They scattered largesse around the local police and officials. They hired gunmen and enforcers.

The godfathers had become so distinctive, they deserved a special term. They were dubbed the *jao pho*. The phrase was a direct translation of "god-father," and may have first been used to translate the title of the Hollywood film. It was also the term for a local spirit lord with extraordinary powers. Both types of *jao pho* operate above and beyond the law.

By the time electoral politics rose in importance in the 1980s, the godfathers were firmly in a position to dominate it. They had money. They had lots of friends and dependents to act as canvassers. They had even more people in their debt. Many, like Chaisiri, were lofted up to parliament. Some others preferred to play the role of kingmaker in the background. A few became so important to electoral success across several provinces that they were made officials of the major political parties. When the police asked provincial officials all over the country to name their local *jao pho*, the list contained over forty MPs.

But while some of the godfathers learned how to strut the national stage, and even talk earnestly about "democracy" and "development," in the background there was always the smell of blood and gunpowder.

Most godfathers had a bullet-proof car. One went further and had a bullet-proof desk. He survived at least one hit by diving behind it when his enemies opened up through the front door. Some like Sia Leng[2] of

---

2. Charoen Pattanadamrongjit, who owns a hotel and other businesses in Khon Kaen, was once reckoned to be one of the largest hosts of the illegal lottery in the country. Although he never entered parliament, he financed many candidates and was influential in national politics in the 1980s. His son, Jakkarin, was elected MP for the Thai Rak Thai Party in 2001 and 2005, and for the People's Power Party in 2008.

Khon Kaen have survived a series of assassination attempts. Others have fallen to assaults by weaponry superior to standard bullet-proofing.

Sia Jiew[3] of Chonburi died in 1991 when his Mercedes was blown off the Bangkok-Pattaya road by a rocket-launcher. In 1989, Sia Yae[4] of Ang Thong was blown up by a claymore mine on the steps of a provincial court house. In 1991, Klaeo Thavikul's[5] car was riddled with automatic gunfire in the Bangkok suburbs.

These were just the more spectacular. In between came a steady stream of bodies dumped by roadsides, right-hand men blasted with Uzis at the regular morning coffee-stall, bombs in cocktail lounges and discos, relatives who disappeared without trace.

Investigating these killings always turned out the same way. The victims had so many business interests, so many potential enemies, so many reasons to be killed, that it was impossible to identify a culprit.

But there are signs that the age of the godfathers is on the wane.

When these killings began in the 1970s, the academic Ben Anderson pointed out that such people were being killed because they were important. Chaisiri's killing is shocking in part because such events have become rarer in the last few years.

Partly this may be simply exhaustion. "I used to have enemies," said one prominent figure in 1990, "but all of them have died." But there are other forces at work.

The extradition of Thanong Siriprichapong to stand trial on drug-running charges in the US was the first time a figure of such stature had been hauled back within the law.[6] The godfathers no longer seemed quite so invulnerable.

---

3. Jumphon Sukparangsi, the most prominent businessman in Chon Buri in the 1970s, and the early patron of Kamnan Poh. "Sia" derives from a Chinese word for a tycoon.

4. Somchai Rerkvararak, who had interests in gambling, construction contracting, and logging. He had survived two earlier assassination attempts, after each of which a prominent rival was gunned down.

5. Klaeo was prominent in gambling and boxing circles in Bangkok.

6. In July 1995, Thanong (Pho Pet) was extradited on charges of having imported 45 tons of marijuana into California.

At the last elections, many of the biggest godfathers decided not to stand. Some like Chaisiri stood but failed. Chaisiri had lost his grip on politics in his own backyard.

When Banharn Silapa-archa rose to the premiership, many predicted a cabinet studded with old godfathers. But so far, Banharn has managed to keep them out.

What is forcing these changes?

The profits of crime are no longer such a large fraction of provincial wealth. More people now make money by more legitimate means. The decline of the military strongmen and better understanding of the secret ballot have made elections less susceptible to old styles of control. Public opinion, crystallized by press and television, has set limits to what is publicly acceptable.

But if the old style of godfather is in decline, is a new style rising in its place? A new style which knows how to manipulate land deeds rather than guns; which knows more money can be made from the stock market than the underground lottery; which can claim to make quick millions by doing "nothing illegal."

This may be the twilight of the old godfathers, but watch out for other evil spirits lurking in the gloom.

MONKS AND GANGSTERS IN THAI POLITICS

6 February 1997

Each democratic system develops its own styles of political leader—styles which command public trust. Many American leaders are modeled on bankers (Roosevelt, Kennedy) or cowboys (Reagan, Clinton). French leaders of both left and right have the manners of the landed gentry (Pompidou, Chirac, d'Estaing). Many British leaders are versions of the neighborhood shopkeeper (Wilson, Heath, even Thatcher). Democratizing Thailand seems to be developing two such styles of leader—the gangster and the monk.

The role of the gangster or tough guy runs back to the feudal lord, the military chief, and the *nakleng*, the village strongman. *Nakleng* were men of action who became powerful through bravery, violence, daring, and gang leadership. They had both good and bad sides. They defended the village against outsiders and dispensed rough justice. But they were easily tempted to use power for gain or sport. They usually adhered to a code of honor. But sometimes this veered into honor among thieves, at the expense of others.

Over a long period of military domination, this *nakleng* role became the dominant style of Thai political leaders. Phibun, Sarit, Thanom, Kriangsak all had this style, as did Sunthorn and Suchinda of the 1991–2 coup regime. Ex-military men like Chatichai and Chavalit also fit the pattern. So do many civilian politicians like Banharn, Montri, Newin, and Snoh.

The *nakleng* style is desperately macho. *Nakleng* leaders revel in macho plumage: military uniforms with lashings of braid and regalia; shiny, brightly-patterned shirts; showy hats (cowboy-style golf hats are a current favorite); chest jewelry and chunky bracelets.

They collect women. Some have well-publicized love affairs. Others are credited by the rumor-mill with multiple liaisons. When Newin

Chidchob was dropping in the popularity ratings, his father told the world that Newin's bony arse made him sexy.

Nakleng drink hard and party hard. Kriangsak is still remembered for his love of fine cognac. Chatichai loved to disco. Suchinda liked whisky, wine, and night-clubs.

Nakleng are sparing with words, and openly skeptical about ideas.

The core principle of *nakleng* leadership is the gang ethic of loyalty and honor. They expect absolute loyalty from their friends and subordinates. In return they must have a "big heart." They must be ready to do anything for a friend or follower. Loyalty and honor override principle. Friendship and connection matter more than justice or fairness.

The alternative political style of the monk has emerged more recently. The most obvious example is Chamlong Srimuang. He was a lay member of an unorthodox monastic cult, and showily adopted many monkish practices. Several other politicians have adopted this style in a more subtle form—most notably the Democrat leader, Chuan Leekpai.

To carry off this style, you have to look a bit like a monk. Chamlong adopted a curious hairstyle half-way between a military crew-cut and a monastic tonsure. Others just look underfed and abstemious. Clothes should be rigorously plain. Chamlong wears a *mohom* peasant shirt or a dull safari suit. Chuan prefers the plainest of white shirts.

Monkish leaders are somewhat distant from women. Chamlong publicly announced that he had given up any sexual relations with his wife. Chuan conducts a liaison which is sexual (there is a child) but not familial (they live apart and are not legally married).

Monkish leaders also need to gain a reputation as good talkers, givers of sermons. Chuan can happily lecture an audience for hours.

These sermons should focus on principle. Chamlong founded his political party on a set of principles of conduct. Chuan talks often about the important of adhering to democratic principles. Both have a reputation for personal honesty that qualifies them to criticize others for corruption and bad behavior.

Anand Panyarachun fits the monkish style but rather imperfectly. He looks trim enough. His wife is rather invisible. He likes to lecture.

He talks a lot about principle. But he spoils things by a fondness for good wine, cigars, and fancy tailoring.

Possibly Anand's failure to adopt the complete monkish style helps explain why he has difficulty winning acceptance among other politicians. During elections to the Constitution Drafting Assembly, Anand was bitterly opposed by politicians who remembered him lecturing them about corruption. In fact, Chuan has lectured MPs on this subject more severely and more often than Anand. But Chuan gets away with it because he is clearly a political "monk," while Anand's style is not so definite.

The most long-standing leader of recent years, General Prem Tinsulanonda, was a unique blend of the *nakleng* and the monk. He acquired *nakleng* style through his military rank and reputation, and embellished it with an affection for brilliant clothing, and ruthlessness in political intrigue. At the same time his style had something of the monk—the ascetic thinness, calm demeanor, absence of female company, and reputation for principle.

But combining the styles like Prem is unusual. More often, they are distinctly separate. Thai political leaders are either *nakleng* or monks. And the two styles tend to be opposed. Chamlong against Suchinda. Chuan against Banharn. Chuan against Chavalit.

The *nakleng* stands for action without principle. The monk stands for principle without action. Sarit, the archetype of the *nakleng* leader, is always remembered as the leader who got things done, though with costs in terms of principle and justice. Chuan is known as a good man, but cannot shake the reputation that he is indecisive and ineffectual.

Here lies the paradox of modern Thai politics. The mass of people believe that good men cannot get things done, and action men cannot get things right.

Very recently there are signs of a new leadership style which tries to get round this paradox.

This new style has roots which are more Chinese than Thai. These roots include the precepts of Sun Tzu, the characters of the *Romance of the Three Kingdoms*, and the stories of Justice Pao. The two key attributes of this new style are strategy and fairness.

First, a good leader of this "Chinese" style is a master at the chess-board strategizing of political in-fighting. He can get things done by cunning.

Second, he dispenses justice with fairness and morality, in spite of pressure from bad men and influential friends.

Banharn and Chavalit both have something of the *nakleng* and something of this new "Chinese" style. Banharn was famous for his political cunning. While other politicians thought two or three moves ahead, it was said Banharn plotted thirty or forty. This may or may not have been true. But his claim to leadership was based in part on the belief that he did. When it came to exercising his power, however, Banharn relapsed to the *nakleng* model of helping friends and followers.

Chavalit was once seen as a poor player of the political chess game. But as he came closer to his goal of the premiership, his reputation for political strategy suddenly increased. He was quickly re-imagined in this "Chinese" leadership style.

Chavalit also wants to present himself as a just ruler, who will not put friendship and loyalty above right and justice. For several years, he has reveled in comparison to Khong Beng, a general in the *Romance of the Three Kingdoms*. Khong Beng solved problems by quick thinking, and acted justly despite fierce pressures. Now Chavalit tells us he will rule well despite the track record of most of his cabinet colleagues. He promises to reform the political system, even though this system brought him to power. He promises to cut the military budget even though he himself is a soldier. He promises to lead a campaign of austerity even though his millionaire ministers love flaunting their wealth.

Monks and gangsters offer us a clear choice—between moral man and action man. The new "Chinese" style of leadership is more ambitious and more slippery. It tells us: trust me, I'm tricky but I have a good heart, and I can work miracles. Remember Banharn "I will not disappoint the people," and Chavalit "I will do my best."

We know now about Banharn. Whether Chavalit is really Khong Beng or just another *nakleng*, we are all about to find out.

CHATICHAI'S STAIRCASE

9 November 1997

Over the last eleven months, as the political play slid from melo-drama, to tragedy, to horror, the principal stage set has been Chatichai Choonhavan's house.[7]

Theater is an intrinsic part of politics. Where kings and nobles once had to stage-manage ceremonial to dramatize their rule, television now dramatizes politics on a daily basis.

In the past, this drama was strictly stage-managed. The nightly news followed an exact hierarchy—the palace, the military heads, the prime minister, other ministers.

In the 1990s, this rigid sequence has disappeared. Yet for some years, television developed no distinctive set-pieces of political theater except the Government House Ambush, in which politicians descend the ornate central staircase of Government House into a thicket of micro-phones, cassette recorders, and video crews.

But this scene lacks an essential element of such theatrical set-pieces—the scope for variety. At first some ministers advanced into the ambush with a swagger, some with obvious fear, some even with a whiff of mischief. But before long most politicians learned how to set their teeth into a smile, wade into the ambush, and bluster. The scene became predictable and boring.

Over the last year, the daily drama of politics has been transformed. We have been let into Chatichai's house. Partly the transformation

---

7. Chavalit Yongchaiyudh headed a coalition government (1996–7) including his own New Aspiration Party along with the Democrats, Chat Thai, Chat Phatthana, and smaller parties. Chatichai Choonhavan, who had been prime minister in 1988–90 but was now semi-retired from politics, offered to help Chavalit manage the coalition. The Chavalit government fell three days before this article appeared.

comes from the house itself. This is Ratchakhru,[8] one of the baronial castles of Thai politics. The camera's sweeps, pans, and zooms convey a sense of space, of grandeur, of investment. This family has been at the center of Thai politics for three generations.

Partly the transformation results from the stage management skills of Chatichai himself. The house provides the setting for at least three major set-pieces which have been played over and over again, with subtle variations of tone and tempo.

1. The Greeting. The sequence and detail of the political *wai* has become almost as complex as the formal Japanese bow. The performance of the two parties is shaped by several variables. Of course, their relative ages matter as in any such greeting. Then the number of seats each controls in the House. And finally the message which each wants to pass to the viewing public. The guest can vary the depth, length, and degree of reverence in his *wai*. The host's response can range from competitive self-abasement, through mere warmth, to polite condescension.

Surely soon we will be treated to action replays and expert analysis, rather like football commentary, with statistics of each participant's depth and length replacing percentage possession and shots on goal.

The Greeting does not end with a single exchange. The aftermath is an intrinsic part of the scene. At one extreme, the host throws a welcoming arm around the guest's shoulders with just a hint of Russian bear-hug. At the other, the couple separates quickly, twisting out of the formal parallelism of the *wai*, avoiding even eye contact.

In Chatichai's hallway, this scene has been extended further. In the crudest variant, the two actors grasp hands and mug for the camera in simulated friendship or shared triumph. In the subtler versions, the couple retreat into the inner recesses of the house with the lens zooming in pursuit. One places a hand on the other's shoulder (friendship, guidance); the two grasp hands (common purpose); heads bend together in an intense private exchange of words (commitment to affairs of state).

---

8. Ratchakhru is a road in Bangkok, slightly north of Victory Monument. In the 1950s the name was given to a powerful political faction centered on several interrelated families (including the Choonhavans) who lived in this district.

The political *wai* is not new. But earlier leaders did not exploit its dramatic potential. Chuan stuck to the politely formal. Banharn, as in so much else, looked as if he was straining to follow an auto-prompt. Chatichai, Chavalit, and their entourages have developed the *mise en scene* of the political *wai* to new levels.

2. *The Private Party Meeting.* Occasionally this scene has been staged with various participants from the coalition, but usually it is confined to the Chat Phatthana party. Members arrive one by one and are ushered into the meeting room on the ground floor. The impact of the scene is achieved by allowing the cameras to set up very close to the meeting room door. We are right there! As each participant arrives, a minder eases open the door a fraction, and allows the guest to slide in. We get a brief glimpse inside, and then the door closes.

This scene is lifted straight from gangster films. What happens as the guest passes inside and the door closes against our view? A password? A masonic sign? A quick check for hardware? The scene reeks of secrecy, magic, conspiracy, power.

This impression is confirmed by the later denouement. As the meeting breaks up, one of the younger party offsiders is deputed to talk to the cameras. He saunters towards the lenses with over-acted casualness. Hands in pockets. Laconic smile. Detached air. He fixes his eyes on the ceiling, and talks over the heads of the cameramen and interviewers: nothing happened in the meeting, nothing was decided, nothing to report. We have been allowed right up to the doorstep, but then elegantly excluded. We are not part of the chosen few. The events behind that narrowly opening door are too important, too exciting for us to know.

3. *The Staircase.* Meetings with party outsiders take place upstairs, beyond The Staircase. Ever since Chavalit consented to Chatichai hosting the coalition's discussions, Chatichai has exploited the staging mercilessly. The spider welcoming the fly. The gods admitting mere mortals for a short-term visit to heaven.

For this scene, the cameras are kept some way back to allow a rising pan shot up The Staircase. Coalition members arrive one by one. The ascent of the lower flight of The Staircase is their chance for a solo performance. Snoh shambles up with tired resignation. Chalerm pirouettes for the cameras. Korn shows off his new shirt. Samak ignores the cameras pointedly and looks the other way. The technocrat ministers tiptoe timidly, heads swiveling to take in the scenery (they may not be back many times).

The Staircase creates a powerful illusion—those who ascend it disappear. First they are foreshortened by the upward perspective. Then they turn the corner and are cut to half by the banister. At the top they are reduced to a head. Then they disappear. Into the heavens. Into the spider's sanctum.

In the early days of the coalition, Chatichai often welcomed Chavalit on the ground floor, and accompanied him up The Staircase in the aftermath of The Greeting (arm around shoulder, hand clasp, whispered exchange). More recently, he has appeared only at the top. A wave from the heavens. A flash of cigar.

All these rehearsals were preparation for the one-performance-only drama of last Monday night.[9] We could tell this was an unusual night because the staging was all wrong. The Greeting scene was dropped completely. Perhaps neither could work out how best to play it. The Private Party Meeting took place off to one side, a little more visible than usual (a show of strength?) but out of earshot (still smugly secret). Chavalit's performance on The Staircase was deliberately bungled. The affair had become a crowd scene. On the way up he seemed lost and confused. On the way down, he was hustled and shielded from view, like a fugitive or a film star feigning a wish for privacy.

This show has had a great run. No encore. No curtain calls.

---

9. The date was 3 November 1997. The government fell three days later.

CHAVALIT AND THE SALWEEN SAGA

13 March 1998

The Salween logging[10] affair is much more than just another chain-saw massacre. Its roots lie in Thai-Burmese relations and the rhythms of General Chavalit Yongchaiyudh's political career.

In 1988 General Chavalit, army commander-in-chief, traveled to Rangoon at the head of a large, top-level military delegation. This visit resulted in a major change in Thai-Burmese relations. Thailand would quietly disassociate itself from the international antagonism to the Burmese military dictatorship, and stop supporting the rebel groups along the border. The price for this support was timber and fishing rights.

Why this change, and why was this part of foreign policy being handled by the army? On the Burmese side, the junta was gearing up to move against its opponents—the democracy movement and the rebel minorities—and it first needed support from Thailand and China. On the Thai side, the army was under intense pressure. Its bloated role in all aspects of government was being whittled back by increasingly confident elected politicians and pressure groups. The businesses (arms buying and construction) that had traditionally financed the generals'

---

10. The Salween logging scandal broke when deputy forestry chief Prawat Thanadkha presented a box containing 5 million baht to the prime minister, claiming that it was a bribe and that he could not think what else to do with it. It soon emerged that logs had probably been illegally felled in Thailand, shipped to Burma, and then returned as imports, or simply made to appear that way in the paperwork. In total, 33,884 logs were seized. In 2005, Prawat was jailed for five years for accepting the bribe, and Vinai Panichayanuban was jailed for two years for giving the bribe. Evidence showed that Vinai withdrew the 5 million from Bank of Ayudhya and delivered it to Prawat who accepted it but then panicked (*Bangkok Post*, 12 November 2005). The scandal resurfaced in 2003 when 100,000 logs were found hidden submerged in Chiang Saen Lake, and some suspected these were related to the scandal. The ownership was traced to Wattana Asawaheme.

taste for Mercedes and other trinkets, were being closed down by public exposure. Burma offered a new frontier—both for business opportunities and political assertion.

As a result of the negotiations, twenty concessions were given to Thai companies for logging inside Burma. Virtually all the companies were owned by military officers and associates. Some of their executives figured among the supporters of the New Aspiration Party which General Chavalit founded a year later. Within months, the Thai government had banned all logging inside Thailand and these Burmese concessions had become hugely valuable.

The Thai army began clearing up the border by shoveling some of the refugee students back into Burma. It stopped when the international press reported that many of these returnees had gone missing, presumably executed. A Burmese army unit was allowed to cross into Thailand and attack a Karen rebel refugee camp. A Thai border town was wasted in the attack. General Chavalit stamped his foot in outrage at this invasion and promised to extract reparations. But nothing happened.

Golden years. As recent reports attest, these were the golden years in Tak and Mae Hong Son. Fortunes were made fast and almost legally. The logging inside Burma faced almost no restriction, and the Thai companies chopped fast and furiously. Burma-watcher Martin Smith saw one forest reserve where 100,000 trees had been cut in one year. The border also bred other lucrative trades—bringing out girls and heroin, and trading in arms for the rebel groups.

But the diplomatic basis of this golden era was shaky. Between 1992 and 1994, it fell apart. International environmental groups and some Burmese voices protested against the scorched-earth clear-cutting by the Thai loggers. On the Thai side, the military's prestige and political weight took another lurch downwards after the May 1992 incident. The Democrat-led government recaptured control over Thai-Burmese relations and took a slightly more conditional attitude towards support for the junta. The Burmese were no longer sure they had a deal.

In 1992–3, the Burmese government revoked the logging concessions and proposed to close the border posts. Although the army might be in retreat, General Chavalit was still in the frame as a minister in the Democrat-led coalition. In 1993, he managed to negotiate with Rangoon to keep the border posts open so timber could still flow out. But in December 1994 Chavalit quit the coalition. The golden age passed into history.

But the wheel of history spins round. In 1995, Chavalit returned as defense minister in Banharn's coalition. Thai-Burmese relations again shot ahead. Construction began on the Yadana pipeline and a road link through Kanchanaburi. The army brokered deals for the Ital-Thai Development Company to enter Burma. A delegation of executives from major Thai companies visited Rangoon to prospect for business opportunities. Burma began to sidle up to ASEAN.

With the assurance of Thai support, the Burmese army upped the pressure on the rebel groups along the border with a mixture of armed attacks and conciliatory treaties. A year ago, in a repeat of 1989, the Thai army stood aside while a Burmese unit attacked three rebel refugee camps inside Thailand. Again, the Thai army began pushing people back across the border until human rights groups protested. And again, Banharn and Chavalit reopened the border passes for timber traffic.

New operators. But it seems the timber business developed very differently from expectations. The military-backed timber firms swung back into operation, but they were outflanked by a group of people who had been mere bit-players in the earlier phase.

This new group changed the economics of border logging. Getting timber out of Burma had become more expensive. The remaining stands were deeper in, and the logistics more complex and risky. But trees have no passports, no nationality. Cutting down Thai trees and passing them off as Burmese promised much larger profits.

They also changed the economics by exploiting the human fall-out of border politics. They hired the rebel refugee Karen inside Thailand as cheap labor and devil-may-care gunmen to intimidate rivals. And they worked through pro-Rangoon Karen to launder Thai logs into Burmese.

Som Chankrajang's career is typical of the *jao pho* (local godfathers) of this last generation. He started out with little education, no money, and a burning desire to be very rich. He worked in a gambling den where he learned (as he endearingly told an interviewer last week) "the only way to win is to cheat." He made his first pile by hard graft in the trucking business. Then he made his fortune in the golden age by acting as an agent for the logging concessionaires. He negotiated with the Karen rebel groups to get the timber out to the border.

His key contact was Bo Mya, the grand old man of the Karen resistance. For almost forty years, Bo Mya had been one of the most commercially minded rebel leaders. He had been dealing with Thai loggers and miners since the 1970s. By 1990, the profits had enabled him to create possibly the most settled and organized of the mini-states on the border. When Rangoon upped the pressure on the rebels in 1994, Some Karen groups chose conciliation. They made a pact with SLORC,[11] and donated troops to help SLORC's mopping-up operations. Bo Mya held out, but became more isolated. To maintain his cashflow, he was ready to give Burmese nationality to Thai logs.

Final link. The final link in the chain were the sawmills, especially that of Vinai Panichyanuban. The logs arrived by several routes: routed through Burma to get Bo Mya's chop; seized by the Forest Industry Organization and then sold off; magicked through the checkpoints with no documentation; and possibly also chopped as Burmese without ever leaving Thai soil.

To disguise the operation, this group appears to have used a corruption strategy like carpet-bombing—dropping tons of cash over a wide area to flatten any potential source of opposition, and to leave no cover for anyone who wanted to risk a protest. If the list taken from Som's relative is what it appears to be, the cash was paid in regular amounts to officials from the police, army, local administration, customs, immigration, forestry, and national parks—ranging from some very top men to the little people who hold open the gates.

---

11. The State Law and Order Restoration Council, the name assumed by the junta headed by General Saw Maung which took power on 18 September 1988. In 1997, the name was changed to the State Peace and Development Council.

But the monopoly attempted by Som, Mya, and Vinai was bound to be vulnerable. The old logging companies were furious at being excluded and undercut on price. Other rebel groups along the border hijacked logs in transit. After Chavalit fell from power, the business was quickly undermined. The Forestry Department obstructed the flow of logs from forest to sawmill. Those managing the business believed they could use money to free up the resulting log jam. Somebody panicked.

Now the border business is like an ants' nest that has been poked with a stick. The army tries to blame the Karen. Bo Mya's men attack the rebel camps. Police, customs, and local officials point fingers at one another. The Forestry Department, which must be used to such scandals by now, adopts the turtle defense strategy of withdrawing into its shell and playing dead.

But there are clearly two very different agendas at work. Some may want to clean up the whole business. But some may simply want to dislodge the Som-Bo-Vinai pirate monopoly, and allow more powerfully backed interests to take over again.

Most chilling of all has been General Chavalit. Last week he exploded with one of those impulsive, unguarded, revealing outbursts which have been the hallmark of his political career. Put up or shut up, he challenged; charge me or stop talking about it.

Charges may be difficult. But it seems clear that the appalling destruction of forests on both banks of the Salween is closely linked to the rhythms of General Chavalit's political career.

THE LAST STAND

24 March 1998

No-confidence debates are like cowboy films.[12] In 1995 we saw *The Indian Siege*: wave upon wave of Indians attacked the weak point in the fort wall (the *SPK 4-01* land scandal)[13] until the fort commander (Chuan) conceded and ran up the white flag. In 1996, we watched *The Secret Weapon*: in mid-debate the attackers suddenly whipped the covers off a deadly new kind of weapon (the BBC[14] wide-bore cannon) and blasted a fatal hole through the cabinet defenses. This was followed by *Turncoats*, in which the suspense hinged around the moment when the defenders would break ranks and start pumping bullets into their own beleaguered leader (Banharn).

Just now we have seen *The Last Stand*. The attackers have been cast into the desert. They are tired, thirsty, disheartened. They know their cause is hopeless, but honor requires they make one last stand. Their ammunition is almost exhausted. Their shots and arrows bounce off the armor-plated target like paper darts. Many bullets ricochet back and wound their own men. Just about the only shots they land are on

---

12. In 1995, the Chuan government was felled after a dramatic no-confidence debate. In 1996, the Banharn government fell after two such debates. These events, televised live, seemed to have replaced the coup as the method of transition in Thai politics. Thus in March 1988, the opposition mounted a no-confidence debate against the Chuan cabinet. But the 1997 financial crisis had clearly changed the rules.

13. Under the Chuan government (1992–5), a new land deed was created, primarily to give temporary title to farmers occupying land which was officially classified as "forest" but in practice was conclusively degraded. Only small farmers were supposed to qualify. Several business people were found to have acquired land under this *SPK 4-01* title, especially in Phuket. Some of these were closely connected to the Democrat Party, including the Phuket MP, Anchalee Thephabut. After a long court case, her husband was stripped of 98 rai of land acquired under the scheme

14. Bangkok Bank of Commerce, which collapsed in 1996 after Democrat MPs had exposed multiple scandals in the bank's management during a no-confidence debate.

the renegades, their old friends who have gone over to the enemy. Even Buster Chalerm makes little impact. His pistol cracks but the shots are all blanks. And at the height of the battle his big weapon misfires. He loses his voice and his missiles fizzle out in plaintive croaks.

Then in the climactic scene, the old Indian-fighter, Samak, clambers out onto the parapet, the sounds of battle fall away, and we know it is time for the film's emblematic soliloquy. He looks battered, battle-worn, bloodied, and bowed. His tongue can still flash like quicksilver, but today it is dulled by the clouds of fate. We knew we could not win, he intones, but we just wanted to see the flag fly and the bugle sound one last time. The battle continues around him, but the camera pulls back and away, and we know the film is over and the credits are about to roll.

Perhaps the best cowboy-film metaphor for current Thai politics is *The Wild Bunch*. For years, the old gun-fighters swept all before them—robbing banks, shooting up opponents, carrying off women, swaggering around the saloons, and squabbling over the spoils. But one day they wake up to find that the world has changed, history has moved on, and they have been transformed from romantic heroes into pitiful relics. The finale is a ritualized annihilation.

In *The Wild Bunch*, the symbol for the historical shift was the coming of the railroad. Here it would be the march of Japanese factories out along all Bangkok's radial roads, and of Western finance houses down Asoke and Silom.

Over the past two years, Samak's facial expression has changed from confident pugnacity to pained, frustrated disbelief. He railed against the international rating agencies, whose down-grades prefigured the financial crisis, for having inauspicious names (Moodys, Poor). He exploded in anger when a young reporter dared to disrupt the photo-call for Chavalit's newly formed coalition by asking: how can you expect the public to accept this lot when it's much the same as the old lot. He lost his temper with the Assembly of the Poor protesters who, in earlier days, would have been dealt with more decisively. He could not brook the popular pressures which shaped the transition from Chavalit to Chuan, and watched his party shatter as a result. He cannot fathom why the media should be allowed so much freedom. He (and many of his allies on the opposition front bench) belong to an age of simpler, more brutal politics—transacted behind closed doors, veiled from public view, backed by guns.

Over the last two years, the Democrats have carefully constructed a public image which is as far away from this old guard as possible. In the second no-confidence debate against Banharn, Chuan held back the senior Democrats, and let the next generation have the floor—young, attractive, polite, elegant, educated, informed, worldly. In this cabinet, both the Democrat party and its allies are studded with old guard–style politicos. But for the most part these types have kept their heads down behind the parapet. In the front-line Chuan has placed the technocrat team at the center (Tarrin, Supachai, Pisit), the internationalist team on the left flank (Surin, Sukumbhand), and the youth brigade on the right (Abhisit, Jurin, Akkapol). The uniform is a white shirt and a sober tie. The regulation mood is responsible, calm, and concerned. No shiny shirts. No chunky jewelry. No public outbursts. A little bland but very wholesome.

After Samak's speech on last Thursday night, the iTV camera ignored the next speaker and stayed on Samak. He shuffled his papers thoughtfully then rose and walked rather heavily out of the chamber. A few nods to colleagues, but no plaudits and no enthusiastic greetings. It was the defining visual image of the debate.

The battle of course is far from over. Old gunslingers never give up because, quite simply, there is no other way of life they know. They will regroup and return to the assault. They will send out snipers, blow up baggage trains, and mine the battlefield.

But their admission of defeat was there in the soliloquy of Samak's last stand. We came out to fight again this time, he explained, because we did not want to be blamed for losing the Battle of the Economy. That loss was the fault of Tarrin and the Democrats back in 1992–5. Probably he continued: our side could not fix it during 1995–7 because we don't have anyone who understands this economics stuff at all. But that part of the speech was lost in the sound of gunfire.

LOOKING FOR KHUN ESTRADA

8 June 1998

In Jakarta, an aristocratic, military-backed dictator is brought down by popular agitation. In Manila, a poorly educated, dissolute ex-film-star is voted in to the horror of the middle class and international observers.

Is this a wind of change blowing through Asia? And will it blow through Bangkok?

Certainly, we are in for some change in political leadership. In the same week as these two momentous events, churchmouse-poor Chuan Leekpai (net family assets: 5 million baht) was accused of leading the rich, while fat-cat Chavalit Yongchaiyudh (net family assets: 1,800 million baht) claimed to lead the poor. Something does seem a little wrong. Thaksin Shinawatra seized the moment to confess he is setting up a party. Meanwhile, the death of Chatichai Choonhavan will—after a respectable delay—set off a lot of banging about in the elephant's grave-yard of Thai politics.

But is Estrada the new Asian model? If we are looking for the next Thai leader, should we forget about Chavalit (the Suharto admirer) and Thaksin (the Daimler donor[15]), and instead go to the movies?

Of course, the Philippines can easily be dismissed as the least typical country of the region—a Latin American state lost in Asia. But the Estrada model is not new. In India, such film-star politicians have been around for decades. The last elections in south India pitted an old matinee-idol against his former leading lady (a bitter contest indeed). The

---

15. Thaksin Shinawatra gave Somboon Rahong a Daimler. Thaksin later explained that Somboon had helped him with contacts in Laos, and though the project did not come off, Thaksin wished to show his gratitude. Thaksin also claimed that he told Somboon not to disclose the gift. Somboon drove the car straight to the parliament car park and told reporters it was a gift from Thaksin.

Philippine and south Indian models are strikingly similar. On film, the stars play roles of gods and heroes of the poor. They right the wrongs which the rich do to the poor, either by macho valor or divine power. Years later, the electors remember these images and vote them in— even though, in the time in-between, they may have grown old, ugly, dissolute, and corrupt.

The prospect of an Estrada-like figure in Thai politics currently seems very remote. There is no sign of an experienced hero-figure movie-star with political ambitions. Sorapong Chatri almost fits the role but seems to have no inclination. Ron Ritthichai plunged into politics but so lacked charisma he lost six consecutive elections before getting a seat in parliament.

Thai politics is dominated by rich plutocrats. The asset declarations showed politicians (with the single exception of Chuan) are a hundred to a thousand times richer than the average man. Thaksin's new party seems founded on the "ideology of money." In this background, an Estrada figure seems unimaginable. But maybe these pluto-politics are exactly the right breeding ground.

So what were the factors behind the rise of star politicians in India and the Philippines? Three things stand out.

First, religious beliefs. In both areas, religion taught people to believe in saints and goddesses which can transform the fortunes of individuals or whole societies through magical power. The Philippines has the redemptive strain of Catholic Christianity. South India has bhakti Hinduism. Both religions taught through stories which made these magical figures almost human. And in the Indian case, the star politicians portrayed these roles during their film careers.

Second, mass media. In both these areas, cinema became hugely popular because it provided villagers with a new and dazzling window onto the outside world. Cinema replaced religious festivals as the outstanding color and drama that provided relief from hard work and poverty.

Third, electoral freedom. These star politicians emerged when the mass electorate suddenly had more freedom to choose. In India they appeared after colonialism had retreated and the fire of nationalism had dulled. In the Philippines, Estrada has risen as Cold-War patronage politics have lost their hold, and the significance of Cory Aquino's revolution has faded.

What then are the prospects for a Thai Estrada?

Rural Thailand certainly has a tradition of religious rebel leaders who claim to turn the world upside down, especially in the north and northeast. History is littered with revolts led by *phumibun* or holy men who promise to overturn the social order and found a heaven on earth. The last instances were recorded in the 1930s. Is this tradition still lurking in the folk memory, waiting to be released by a new-style political savior?

The coming of cinema does not seem to have been such a dramatic event in rural Thailand. And the Thai cinema does not seem to have been so fascinated with poor-avenging-rich Robin Hood figures, or with gods and goddesses who turn the world upside down.

But maybe cinema is the wrong place to look. The important element is the transforming power of mass media, which can make a star into both a magically glamorous figure and at the same time everybody's friend or neighbor. Elsewhere in the developing world, mass electorates have picked pop stars, sportsmen, beauty queens, even poets. Thailand may not have the same sort of cinema as India and the Philippines. But it is certainly star-struck.

On the third point, the Thai rural electorate certainly seems close to the point of release. In the past, rural voters were trussed up by the patronage ties of the local bosses, and cowed by the establishment's fear of any rural organization which shows independence and assertiveness. These obstacles have begun to dissolve. With the education reforms made almost a decade ago, the educational profile of the rural electorate is set to change rapidly. Even more important, the partial liberalization of the electronic media has given rural people access to a political education—through the daily TV news, and the dramatic coverage of no-confidence debates, the passage of the new constitution, and leadership crises. The financial crash has begun to undermine the stultifying myth of urban superiority. And finally, the new constitution and election rules will change the success factors in poll contests.

The next election is perhaps too soon to expect a change. But if we are looking to spot the leader of the early twenty-first century, maybe we should stop comparing the bank balances of telecom tycoons, scouting the family trees of Soi Ratchakhru, and urging Abhisit to grow up quickly. Perhaps instead we should be sifting through the faces on the game shows, the *luk thung* stages, and the TV soaps.

MONTRI PONGPANIT: LEST WE FORGET

2 November 1998

Montri Pongpanit's decision to step down from the leadership of the Social Action Party (SAP), and from the cabinet, is a historic moment. Since 1988, with Montri as general secretary and then leader, SAP has been part of *every* elected coalition government. In most of them, Montri has occupied a senior ministerial post. No other party or leader can match this record of staying in power.

But what have the people got out of this? Montri himself hardly ever says a word in parliament. He has never aired any vision on the future of Thailand or the role of democracy. He has not been identified with any significant piece of legislation. Meanwhile Chang Noi has several times heard Montri nominated as candidate for the title of "the worst man in Thailand."

In 1990, when SAP was a partner in Chatichai Choonhavan's "buffet cabinet," an SAP junior minister under pressure to resign over corruption charges decided to sing to the press about the wrongdoings of his colleagues. In particular, he described how Montri, as party secretary-general, had tutored him on how to accept bribes, as follows: "In what you do, be sure there is a perfect fit [i.e. no loose ends], that all is clear. Have them come and meet you and write the numbers on a paper, and tear it up and throw it away. Don't go and say for that a million, for this a million." After the junior minister was forced to admit he held stock in a construction company which his ministry had awarded a contract, Montri had upbraided him: "How can you have stock [in the construction company]? I have a lot [of stock in similar situations] and don't see any problems. Use the names of subordinates."

The junior minister concluded: "Montri taught me the techniques to make money for the party. I am not as good as Montri ..." *The Nation* ran the story under the headline "Montri taught me to cheat."

Others came forward to confirm that Montri was expert in these techniques. Another MP told how Montri had given him a check for 40,000 baht to settle a problem, but when the issue got into the press, Montri asked him to return the check in return for 40,000 baht in cash wrapped up in a newspaper.

In the Chatichai government (1988–91), Montri held the post of minister of transport and communications. After he signed a contract for installation of 3 million new telephone lines at a cost of 150 billion baht, the press alleged major bribery had taken place. The successor Anand Panyarachun government called for a revision on grounds that the agreement broached contract law. As part of the revision, the contractor's profit was reduced by 70 billion baht.

In the dying days of the Chatichai government, five contracts were signed for transport projects in Bangkok, under the control of various ministries. Montri signed the deal with Hopewell.[16] The rumor-mill told of agents visiting ministers with suitcases full of cash to secure the vital signatures before the government fell. Nobody cared to notice that the various projects were mutually incompatible in many ways. Sorting out the mess delayed these projects for years.

After the 1991 coup, Montri was one of the ten people found to have become "unusually wealthy" during the Chatichai government. According to the Assets Examination Committee, he had profited to the extent of 336.5 million baht, particularly from the inflated price on a land purchase by Thai International. This figure was the second highest, exceeded only by the SAP minister of commerce who had garnered 608 million in gift checks from agricultural exporters. The committee was later deemed unconstitutional so the verdicts lapsed.

In a Chulalongkorn University survey in 1992–3, 37.9 percent of people cited SAP in reply to the question "thinking of corruption what political party do you think of," ranking SAP second behind Chat Thai.

---

16. A mass transit scheme, promoted by the Hong Kong entrepreneur, Gordon Wu. The project collapsed after the 1997 crisis, leaving a trail of unfinished concrete pillars across the city.

In the Banharn Silapa-archa government (1995–6), Montri was minister of agriculture. In May 1996, an opposition MP alleged that he had made 2 billion baht from a scheme to distribute fertilizer to poor farmers. The price, the MP contended, was inflated and many sales took place on paper only. The same MP also suggested Montri had profited from sale of machinery to a state enterprise under the ministry. He described how the contractor and ministry representatives had haggled over the bribe by silently exchanging hand signals, with each finger raised signifying 1 million baht.

Montri also backed the construction of the Kaeng Sua Ten dam. Opponents claimed the project offered more benefits to contractors and bribe-takers than to the farmers, and would destroy the nation's last remaining forest of golden teak. Montri countered that this teak forest simply did not exist. Newspapers published photos to disprove him. One paper ran a cartoon portraying Montri as a caped Dracula with his fangs sunk into a tree. Banharn switched Montri to a deputy premiership before these allegations had time to ferment.

In the Chavalit Yongchaiyudh government (1996–7), Montri was minister of health. No scandal emerged during his tenure, but doctors and health officials recently insisted that the ministry should be removed from SAP as two ministers had already done so much damage.

Montri's reputation has rubbed off on his junior SAP colleagues. Somsak Thepsuthin and Rakkiat Sukthana have become lightning rods for corruption allegations. During the Banharn cabinet, Somsak was a deputy communications minister. The press alleged he profited from irregularity in buying computers for the meteorology department. Just before the government fell, he signed a contract for landfill at the Nong Ngu Hao airport. The press and Amnuay Virawan later alleged the price was vastly inflated. As industry minister in the Chuan Leekpai cabinet (1997–8) Somsak became an early target for corruption allegations, particularly over an alleged 200 million baht bribe to raise sugar prices.

During the Banharn government, Rakkiat Sukthana was minister in the Prime Minister's Office. When he sacked the entire board of the electricity generating authority (EGAT), union members alleged he was planning to fix the bidding on a power plant project. Under Chuan, he has been at the center of the scandal in the health ministry.[17]

Of course, all these allegations may be without any substance. Nothing has been legally proven. Except in the "unusually wealthy" investigation, no receipts have been found. But it is still a remarkable history.

Montri's success in staying close to power has been based on a very canny formula. Alone among the leaders of major parties in recent years, he has shown no ambition to become prime minister. As a result, he has not crashed and burned as others have. Instead, he has offered SAP to every successive prime minister as a nice little coalition filler. This in turn has enabled him to attract a continuing supply of new party recruits who have seen SAP as one of the most reliable routes to a ministerial post.

He has glided from coalition to coalition with the grace of a figure-skater. In 1991, he was branded by the military as one of the "unusually wealthy" of the Chatichai era. But by early 1992, he made his peace with the generals and was accepted into the military-led coalition. When this coalition appeared doomed, he publicly turned critical and two months later slid into the anti-military "angel" coalition under Chuan. Similarly in 1996 he slid from Banharn to Chavalit with ease, and from Chavalit to Chuan with only a little bumpiness.

Montri has increased his appeal as a coalition filler by not competing for the high-profile ministerial posts. He and his party have shown little interest in the finance, interior, or foreign portfolios. After the high-profile high jinks of the Chatichai era, he has even steered clear of communications. Instead he has focused on health and agriculture. Usually they attract little public attention. But of course they have large procurement budgets.

In face of the flood of allegations that have come his way over the last decade, Montri's response has been similarly low-key. He has not indulged in showy professions of innocence. He has not hurled law-

---

17. For which he was convicted and sent to jail, a unique example of a minister who has been punished in this way. Somsak is still at large.

suits about. Rather, he has kept his head down. And occasionally moved himself and his people discreetly out of the firing line.

Montri's professed stepping-down from the political front-line may only be a feint. But there is a feeling that he really is ready for retirement, and that SAP is doomed. So it is important to mark this historic moment, and to record the background. Lest we forget.

ACHAN JI SETS KHUN SAMAK A HISTORY EXAM

26 June 2000

Every few months, the events of 1973 or 1976 flash back into the news. Now it is Ji Ungpakorn's call for Samak Sundaravej to admit his role in the 1976 massacre. A few months ago, it was the controversy over a school textbook covering the events of 1973. Further back, Chuan was challenged for approving a decoration for Thanom Kittikhachon, the last of the dictator-generals. Before that, the issue was over a monument to the democracy martyrs. And back to 1996, the emotional commemoration of the twentieth anniversary of the 1976 events.

The veterans of 1973–6 have matured in age and risen in influence. Their generation is now at its prime. Look at the top ranks of many institutions in Thailand today, and you find them. In the cabinet and parliament. Among top figures in the media. In the ranks of professors and teachers. On the boards of leading companies. They are found almost everywhere you don't have to wear a uniform.

If Thailand today has democracy, press freedom, and human rights, then that is the result of these historical events. Need proof of that claim? Look at Thailand's Southeast Asian neighbors. In Indonesia, the process of removing the dictators has only just begun, one generation later. In Burma, it has been blocked, with awful results. Other neighbors are effectively one party states with (at best) carefully managed parliaments and very limited freedom of speech. Thailand's democracy and human rights—imperfect as they are—did not arise by accident or by the drift of history. They were won on the streets through incidents which shifted the course of history, changed people's lives and mindsets, and left behind a cost.

But then there's a big question. How come the society seems so reluctant to recognize this truth? How come it won't embrace this history, and be proud of it?

These issues were laid out in the controversy over the Education Ministry's proposed school textbook about the 1973 events. The historian, Charnvit Kasetsiri, was a member of the committee to review the book's draft. In his review, he set the Education Ministry a little exam. Q1: How come the ministry asked a poet to write this book rather than a historian? The verses decorating the text were a lot better than the text itself. Q2: How come the book was not based on primary sources? Much of the narrative was plainly wrong. Q3: How come a son-in-law of one of the generals brought down by the 1973 events was a co-member of the review committee? He can hardly be disinterested. Q4: How come we need such "authorized" textbooks? Maybe it's time for a more free market in historical knowledge for schoolchildren.

Behind all of Charnvit's exam questions was one big query: is this an attempt to open up the truth, or to keep it buried?

Despite these limitations, the events of 1973 are at least creeping towards the light. Those of 1976 are still much more deeply plunged in darkness. In a famous piece on the growth of Thailand's constitutional democracy, Anand Panyarachun acknowledged the importance of 1973 and 1992, but slid past 1976 as if the year was not in the calendar. Nobody is talking seriously about a textbook on 1976.

1976 is much more difficult to manage for two main reasons. It was much more violent. Some of those involved in unleashing the violence are still alive and still important today.

Of these, Samak Sundaravej is one of the most prominent. Hence Achan Ji Ungpakorn's little exam for him. Q1: Did he back the radio station which was screaming "Kill them, kill them" on the eve of the massacre? Q2: Did he claim the Thammasat students were working for the Vietnamese communists? Q3: Did he, basically, approve?

The answers to this exam are easy. Samak's major role in these events is well-known.

Through late 1976, he was instrumental in splitting the centrist parliamentary coalition which was trying to control the slide towards polarization and violence. To cabinet colleagues at the time, it seemed he was acting like a spoiler, probably on behalf of military friends. He spoke in cabinet justifying General Thanom's furtive return from exile, which triggered the endgame. The centrists' counter-maneuver to drop Samak from the cabinet on 5 October led directly to the awful events on the following day.

After the horrific violence had taken place, he helped build an argument to justify it: that the students were led by or manipulated by Vietnamese communists engineering the overthrow of the country. This began on the day of the massacre itself. The authorities spread rumors that armed Vietnamese were inside Thammasat. A dead body was identified as Vietnamese on the evidence of an amulet with writing that "might be Vietnamese." Dr. Puey Ungpakorn recorded all of this in the memoir written after he was forced to flee in fear of his life. His son, Ji, claims to have heard Samak repeat these rumors when speaking overseas.

Samak could easily answer the questions and pass with full marks. It wouldn't harm his chances in the Bangkok mayor election at all. Instead he has responded with a libel suit. This knee-jerk reaction betrays his admiration for the less-than-democratic states among Thailand's neighbors. He accuses Ji of working for one of his rivals. Since there is only one significant rival, does Samak think the unreformed socialist Ji is working for the capitalist doyenne, Sudarat?

More importantly, Samak asks his own question: why bring all this up now? It's history. It's a generation ago.

But Ji is part of that history. Not simply is he the son of a father who was one of the most poignant victims of the 1976 events. But he has resurfaced in Thailand complete with the courageous outspokenness which his father used to taunt and shame the dictators. He proudly embraces the socialism which many hope had passed into history. In an age when ideology has become unfashionable, he is a startling and important voice.

His challenge to Samak hides an unspoken question. How come someone who opposed the transition from dictatorship to democracy should benefit from this transition, while so many supporters suffered martyrdom or exile? Samak's career now is on the slide. Indeed, it has been all downhill since he was interior minister in the post-1976 government, which was so reactionary even the army was embarrassed. But still, Samak wants one more democratic triumph. Ironically he is contesting an election which he himself banned when he had the dictatorial power to do so.

Samak's response to Achan Ji's exam deserves an F. But he's not the first or last to fail. The events of 1976 won't leave Samak or anyone else alone because it's history that has not been allowed to rest. Thongchai Winichakul called it "a ghost from the past in our mind." As long as it cannot be discussed, absorbed, settled, then the ghost will continue to walk through the nation's public conscience at regular intervals.

DRINKING WITH MR. PROGRESS

23 July 2001

Traveling into Thailand's remoter regions has one special reward. You drive a long way down a dirt road. Better still, you walk for hours away from towns, roads, and telephone wires. At nightfall, your village hosts produce a flagon of *lao khao*, *sattho*, or *khachae*—local liquor. They ask you to sample. They want to know if you like it. It's their handiwork. It comes from a traditional local recipe.

Your hosts take you to see the production. The technique is simple, but they are proud of the expertise. The same equipment was described by seventeenth-century visitors to Ayutthaya. You can see it in use outside Luang Prabang in Laos, in Sipsongpanna in China, and elsewhere.

You have no problem in giving your hosts the praise they want. Chang Noi has sampled brews in Chiang Rai, Mae Hong Son, and Sakon Nakhon which are outstanding. Smooth. Herbally fragrant. More of a wine strength than a spirit. Full of good feeling.

But with one tiny drawback: totally illegal.

If you want a legal, affordable tipple, you have a limited choice among products made from the waste products of sugar mills. They are little different from industrial alcohol. Recently Thailand has also been importing cheap whisky considered virtually undrinkable in its country of origin. A lot of rural Thai men die prematurely in their forties because their stomachs fall apart. Some believe there might be a connection.

Remote places have always defied the liquor laws. But over recent decades, places have become much less remote. Subterfuge has become more difficult. Villagers in Phrae fought gun battles with excise officials to protect their local liquor industry. This defiance has now become more widespread. Villagers besiege police stations to rescue arrested distillers. In May, ten thousand attended a two-day festival of local liquor in Chiang Rai. The producers formed an association and handed out membership cards. Last month, they held a "seminar" in prestigious Chulalongkorn University at the heart of Bangkok.

While the liquor laws make a lot of people frustrated, they make one man staggeringly rich: Mr. Progress.[18]

For two hundred years, the government has raised revenue from liquor through tax farms and licensed monopolies. Making profits under such arrangements has nothing to do with the normal laws of business competition. You make more profit by fooling the customer and fooling the tax-gatherer.

Mr. Progress first got into the business by marrying the daughter of the firm which made the bottle caps. In his first venture, he and a partner secured a monopoly for a small and unattractive area, hired the Mekong blender to make a copycat product, and quietly leaked their product across the borders of their concession area into more attractive markets outside. Then in 1983 they bid an outrageously high amount to secure the Mekong concession. Two years later, in their most brilliant maneuver, they went bankrupt.

The banks could not afford to see a billion baht loan go bad. The government could not sacrifice 8 percent of its revenue. So the banks and government put together a monopoly cartel in order to save themselves. Mr. Progress never looked back. He streamlined production to eliminate costs. He separated the production and distribution companies to minimize the tax. He organized the cartel with a hundred-plus cross-owning companies tangled enough to bamboozle any auditor. He folded into the cartel anyone who threatened to compete. By the mid 1990s, gross revenues were estimated at 50 billion baht a year, and Mr. Progress's share in the cartel was an estimated 55 percent.

The profits are huge. Mr. Progress reinvests them heavily, not in improving the product, but improving his protection. General Prem, who was prime minister when he secured the first concessions, became

---

18. In 2005, *Forbes* magazine ranked Charoen Sirivadhanabhakdi 194th among the world's billionaires with assets of 120 billion baht (around US$3 billion). "Charoen" translates as "progress."

a chairman of one of his companies. General Chatichai and members of his 1988–91 cabinet, which renewed the cartel's concession without competitive bidding, were found to have received 900 million baht in gift checks from Progress companies. General Suchinda came to the premiership vowing to dislodge Mr. Progress, but reputedly fell under his charms. General Chavalit is a long-time associate. According to rumor, Mr. Progress's annual "public relations" budget is 2 billion baht. That would go a long way, even among generals. It would go even farther among government officials who make and administer the liquor rules.

In the late 1990s, government announced it would liberalize the liquor market. Mr. Progress did not let such a profitable monopoly go without a fight. He tried to buy all the glass factories so competitors could not get bottles. He bought the land circling some distilleries so competitors could not get into them. He stockpiled so much tax-paid liquor that he could flood any competitor out of the market. In 1998, the cabinet liberalized the market, but the Excise Department made rules insisting any producer needed 10 million baht capital, 200 rai of land, and a capacity of 30,000 liters/day.

Mr. Progress gives lots to charity. He has been granted an elegant surname. His wife is a Khunying. Both like to be addressed as "Dr.," courtesy of Chiang Mai University. He is blessed by the elite. He lost a bank and a few other trinkets in the crisis, but has still been described as "richer than god." Chang Noi once heard him give a very pretty speech as prologue to a business negotiation. He said his guiding principle was never to enter any business venture unless it was for the good of the nation.

An excise official in Chiang Rai recently said villagers could not be allowed to produce their excellent local liquor because "it wouldn't be fair to large distillers." Let's turn that round. Overthrow the excise rules which allow Mr. Progress to make unfair profits at the expense of village distillers. Chang Noi would drink to that. Preferably in *lao khao*.

THE TRIALS OF KAMNAN POH

28 April 2003

It must be quite a shock. One week you are a big wheel. You generously offer a huge bit of land to the government. You are in line to grab the big plum, Thailand's first legal casino. Your son is a minister. If you call a party, half the country's political elite comes. Then next week, you have a five-year jail sentence, you face a murder charge, and the Anti-Money Laundering Office is panting to seize your assets.

Kamnan Poh's[19] name is a synonym for "godfather" and "influence." For fifteen years, every journalistic review and academic study on Thailand's murky local politics has made him the star.

This is not because he has been the biggest or baddest of them all. Rather, he has been the proudest and the most confident. His rise was spectacular. Fisherman. Smuggler. Land dealer. Local politician. Big national political wheel. It's a great story and Kamnan Poh has enjoyed telling it. Of course he edited out a lot. But what he left in the accounts was breathtaking. Who else could say, "I used to have enemies in Chon Buri, but they all died"? Over the past decade, he has seemed ever more secure, confident, and untouchable. A senior police officer, deputed by the prime minister to investigate Poh, reported being hauled off the case by the top man in the police hierarchy. That is influence.

So why has he suddenly run into trouble? His aides suggest it's just a hitch in the bargaining process over the casino deal. That could be true. But there's a larger context, too.

The godfathers rose at a time when there was not a lot of law or government in the provinces. They made lots of money by exploiting that space. And then they provided the law and government. They regulated who got the good deals. They got rid of people who made trouble. They helped out those in difficulty. When big people like ministers,

---

19. Somchai Khunphloem.

generals, or senior bureaucrats came down from Bangkok, they went straight to the godfather to get things done. This was when the term "influence" came into vogue.

Then in the 1980s, parliamentary politics offered the godfathers a way to launder themselves and to upgrade themselves—a broader range of contacts, some bigger deals, and higher status. But it also had a downside. It bought them into contact with a very different system of law and government which claimed to be superior. This started a period of uneasy transition. They were still very powerful—in fact more powerful than ever. But they had to put up with a lot of flak. "Influence" was now modified to "dark influence." Journalists portrayed them as semi-outlaws. Policemen were occasionally sent to hound them. A few got caught and a few retired.

Their survival strategy was to go legit, and to promote their sons. But this was not easy. Other countries have been through this change from a lawless environment for business and politics to a much more regulated one. Think of the transition in the US from the Kennedy patriarch to his presidential son. But in Thailand, it happened much faster. The Thai godfathers had little more than a decade. They had to bring their sons on quickly. They had to settle the blood feuds stretching back over many years and many killings. They had to get out of the bad businesses while preventing another apprentice godfather slipping into their place.

If Kamnan Poh is brought down, he can curse the 1997 Constitution and the economic crisis. The modern politicians from Bangkok want to clean up the godfathers. They want politics and politicians to have a better public image. That means cutting out the people and practices that bring politics into disrepute. The modern businessmen from Bangkok want to clean up the godfathers, too. Only a few years ago, the head of a big Bangkok business dynasty was furious that he had to go cap-in-hand to Kamnan Poh before he could start a business in Chon Buri.

The 1997 Constitution has rigged the political system in favor of the capital. The economic crisis has persuaded the big Bangkok businessmen they need to be in politics. This has swung the balance of power against the godfathers. A few days ago, Thaksin warned politicians to get out of organized crime. Previous prime ministers might have had the same thought, but none came out and spoke it. The warning is a measure of the growing power and confidence of Thaksin and what he stands for—the marriage of big business and government.

But for Thaksin, the timing is delicate too. The last election felled some of the godfathers, but far from all of them. Many are still members of his coalition. One more general election could change the complexion of parliament further, and reduce this problem to insignificance.

But meanwhile, the godfathers are still powerful in their own backyards. Kamnan Poh is admired and liked for the way he ran and developed his hometown. The godfathers are still to a large extent the law and government in the locality. Thaksin's strategy is to court a new sort of popularity through his public leadership style, his populist policies, and his proven ability to get things done. Now that the Democrat Party has committed hara-kiri, Thaksin's popularity at this level is unchallenged. He is dreaming aloud about winning all five hundred seats. But we don't yet know how this national popularity stacks up against the local popularity of the godfathers. At present, it's not an issue. The two are aligned together.

But if Thaksin openly challenges the godfathers, that will change. Nidhi Eoseewong once argued mischievously that Thai people support local "influence" in order to counterbalance the "power" of the central government. Will that be the story of the next election? Or will Thaksin have bypassed the godfathers? We have to wait two years to find out. Will that be too long for Kamnan Poh?[20]

---

20. No and yes. At the 2005 elections, the old godfathers flooded back under the TRT Party. Three of Kamnan Poh's sons became MPs. Yet in 2006, Kamnan Poh was found guilty in two cases: for profiting from selling land to a public institution, and for masterminding the shooting of an enemy during a marriage ceremony. Just before the appeal verdict on the murder case, Kamnan Poh disappeared. Some believe he is in Cambodia. Others suspect he still lives close to his old home in Chon Buri.

THE LION OF SONGKHLA

31 January 2005

In the tape transcript claimed to have been recorded in Songkhla, some-one addressed as "minister" proposes "we buy everything everywhere" to overtake poll rivals. He concedes, "sometimes our own relatives can-not be bought," but urges his listeners to be bold. He will leave Baht 100,000 with the governors and they can pick it up one day after the poll "if we win." He adds, "we'll worry about the yellow and red cards later," and rounds off: "get the winning votes, then come to collect the money from the governors, and go celebrate."

Of course, nothing is proved. Newin Chidchob, alleged to be the minister involved, is threatening law suits. The prime minister says, "The opposition appears to be very good at playing politics." An elec-tion commissioner claims he cannot decipher the audio recording even though newspapers have transcribed it word for word. The Demo-crats have slipped up before by being too hasty to make use of flaky evidence.

But a police colonel and local election official was present and is prepared to testify. Moreover, the incident fits a pattern from past elec-tions. Remember a certain Chat Thai minister urging his lieutenants to pile on the "ammunition" in the last days before the 2001 poll?

In truth, there are only two aspects of this incident which are impor-tant. The first is the role of the governors. If it is true that the "minister" expected the governors to act as paymasters in this exercise of whole-sale vote-buying, it suggests how much the bureaucracy has become a department of the ruling TRT Party. The second is the role of Newin Chidchob.

Whether the Songkhla incident is true or a set-up, Newin is the perfect choice for the lead character because of his history. In 1995, police raided a Buriram shophouse and found 11.3 million baht in small denomination notes, some of them stapled to a campaign flyer for the

Chat Thai slate led by Newin. These facts are not in doubt, nor (for most people) is the interpretation. But the election law is rather like the prostitution law. Judges will not convict unless police catch the client both engaged in the act and paying the money at the same time, which is technically a bit difficult for both the client and the police. In the Buriram case, judges convicted the shophouse owner, but not those who put up the money or profited from its use.

Newin's name also came up when representatives of a Japanese firm were physically prevented from submitting a bid for a construction contract won by Newin's father-in-law. Again, Newin was not too embarrassed.

At the foundation of TRT in 1998, Thaksin said his goal was to rid Thai politics of "professional politicians" who used money to gain political power and used political power to make money. For many observers, that description would seem to include Newin. Yet, over the last few years, Newin has become one of Thaksin's bluest-eyed boys. Newin was lured to defect from Chat Thai to TRT along with his local faction. He was initially excluded from the cabinet because of his reputation, but has then been a minister continuously since March 2002. He was at the forefront of the great cover-up over bird flu, but was defended from having to take the consequences. He is not standing for election but is tipped as a ministerial candidate after the coming poll.

In short, over the past four years, Thaksin's patronage has helped to launder Newin from being one of Thailand's most *yi* (yucky) politicians into someone almost establishment. If the Songkhla allegations are true, this has not happened because Newin's political ethics have changed. What is new is that his skills are now being put to work for the TRT Party. Was he sent to help the TRT's campaign in the south— the most difficult region for the party—precisely because of what he is good at?

Of course, in politics there is always a tension between what has to be done to gain power, and how that power might be used. By the time of the 2001 elections, Thaksin had stopped presenting himself as a new broom sweeping the old trash out of Thai politics, and instead hoped he could act as "the link between the old generation of politicians and the new." Things have now gone much farther. TRT is beginning to look quite "old."

In 2001, several of the old local boss politicians missed the TRT boat. Perhaps they failed to predict TRT's spectacular rise. Perhaps they believed Thaksin's earlier claims that the party was not for the likes of them. As a result, several of them lost at the 2001 polls. Things are different today. The TRT's candidate list for 2005 is a roster of the great local bosses, their families, and their friends.

Some had made it into TRT before 2001 (Snoh Thienthong's faction). Some were acquired by the merger of other parties into TRT. Many others, like Newin, have defected as individuals or factions. However they arrived, the pattern is now clear. Three Thienthong candidates in Sa Kaeo. Three Khunploem in Chon Buri. Angkinan in Phetchaburi. Lik in Kamphaeng Phet, Khamprakob in Nakhon Sawan, Wongwan in Phrae, Thancharoen in Chachoengsao, Kitthithanasuan in Nakhon Nayok, Pattanadamrongjit in Khon Kaen, etc., etc.

In the northeast, for example, 109 of the TRT's 136 candidates are sitting TRT MPs. Of those, twenty-seven defected from another party into TRT before 2001. Another forty-one were acquired by the merger of the New Aspiration, Seritham, and Chat Phatthana parties. Another eight defected from Chat Thai, and one from the Democrats. At least another three lost at the last election under another party banner. TRT has become a big magnet.

Probably Thaksin believes that his personal popularity and his grip on TRT make him a lion-tamer who can keep all these lions under control. But a lion-tamer still has to feed the lions.

Feeding habits

THE POLICE AND THE GOLDEN PIG

14 December 1996

In mid 1996, a Chulalongkorn University team released preliminary findings from a research project on Thailand's illegal economy. The findings included the allegation that Bangkok has many illegal gambling dens or "casinos" which make regular payoffs to the police.

The police reacted with unusual force. Bangkok police station heads proposed to lay complaints against the researchers in all seventy-five of Bangkok's stations. Some officers totally denied the existence of any casinos in Bangkok. The police director admitted that they had existed once, but claimed they had now been cleaned up. One station head appeared in television interviews and radio talk shows dismissing the findings as "not research."

The police campaign went beyond denial. Complaints were filed against one researcher, Sangsit Piriyarangsan, in over twenty stations (such multiple filings are a common technique for harassment). Plainclothes police appeared at the researchers' faculty. Several uniformed squads camped outside Sangsit's house to offer "protection." Death threats and pictures of bullets were sent to the research group's fax machine.

In an extraordinary move, the prime minister stepped in to negotiate a peace. The researchers admitted the study was "incomplete." The police reinterpreted this word as "incorrect," and agreed to back off.

Usually the police are so confident of their power, they simply shrug off criticism. Over the last few years, there have been several commissions of enquiry criticizing the police and demanding reform. Every time, the police have brushed them aside. During the Saudi jewels scandal, the public was shown how gangs of policemen robbed the robbers, and then fought and killed one another over the loot. No senior policeman seemed to think this revealed any deep-seated problem in the force. Some Thai newspapers run regular columns about police malpractice. The police simply ignore them.

Perhaps the fact that the information on police rake-offs from gambling was based on research, and came from a prestigious university, made the police more sensitive. But then again, this is not the first time this Chulalongkorn group has published research critical of the police. In 1993, they published a survey showing police at the top of a list of government units reckoned to be most corrupt. The research also went into great detail about the illegal fees collected by the police, the systems for distributing these fees within the force, and the sums officers pay to get senior posts. When journalists challenged the police director general to react to these findings, he laughed it off. Mere academic research. Not significant.

But on this occasion, the mention of casinos seemed to touch a nerve.

In early December, the Chulalongkorn team presented the final research findings at a public seminar. Sangsit's paper estimated that the police revenue from Bangkok gambling dens was up to 2.77 billion baht a year.

Many police attended the seminar. They listened carefully and took many notes. The station head who had led the mid-year campaign talked directly with Achan Sangsit, and afterwards Sangsit told the press that the two "now understand one another well." The research was now "complete," unchanged in essence, and widely reported in the press. The police seemed to have regained their talent for shrugging it off.

Then along came the Golden Pig.

Pol Maj-Gen Seri Temiyavej[21] is well-known as one of the few senior police officers prepared to speak about police corruption, and about the relations between the police and Thailand's gangsters and godfathers. He told the Chulalongkorn seminar that Bangkok's most famous gambling dens run by Chat Taopoon and Po Pratunam had recently been eclipsed by a much larger establishment, the Golden Pig, run by the wife of a senior police officer in northern Bangkok. She had been

---

21. Now Seripisuth Temiyavej, ex-director general of police.

an enthusiastic gambler herself, and had recently decided to move into the management side of the business. The Golden Pig, Seri claimed, operated under full police protection right down to the guards at the gates.

A golden pig is a symbol of prosperity. A popular version shows the pig wallowing voluptuously in a slurry of golden coins.

The police director quickly denied that the Golden Pig existed. Under press questioning, Seri repeated the information three times, but added that the establishment had probably now disappeared into thin air. Senior police officers and the minister of interior stated that Seri had shown "bad discipline" in making such allegations.

With Sangsit in June and Seri in December, the police have reacted with aggressive denials. But the police have a credibility problem. It is clear many people believe the allegations about the police and gambling dens.

During the mid-year incident, the Council of University Rectors, National Research Council, lawyers association, trade unions, human rights groups, students, and slum-dwellers came out to support the researchers. A television station poll found 9-to-1 in favor of the academics and against the police. People phoned in to talk shows to give the addresses of gambling dens near their homes and the days on which the police made their regular calls.

At the Chulalongkorn group's recent seminar, a respected senior civil servant asked the police present to look into a gambling den in his own condominium.

Yet the response of the police is to deny the allegations, and to set up a committee to investigate Seri, not the possible existence of gambling dens.

There is a broader dimension to all this. The Chulalongkorn research suggests that the illegal economy is a root cause of some of the big problems of the day—the huge amounts of money available for vote-buying; the number and prominence of godfather figures; the poor standard of many public services; the rising rate of crime; and the growing role of Thailand as an international center of criminal networks. The fact that illegal activities are allowed to flourish is not the result of some cultural tolerance. Rather, these activities are protected by powerful people, including senior police officers.

Most people are inclined to believe accounts of police corruption, simply because it accords with their own personal experience. Many have had to pay a few hundred baht to policemen for traffic offenses. Others pay more regularly for a vending site. Some are heavied for protection fees. It is all too easy to imagine bigger people paying bigger sums to bigger policemen.

Few doubt that gambling really is a "golden pig," a source of abundant prosperity, for senior officers.

On the other hand, nobody believes that *all* police are corrupt. Again this is grounded on personal experience. Most people have had to deal with police officers who seem straightforward, helpful, dutiful. At the seminar, one police officer reckoned that only 2 percent of police officers are corrupt, but admitted that this fraction is concentrated in the upper ranks.

The minister of interior has complained that Seri's remarks will damage the image of the police. But there is overwhelming evidence that the image is very bad already. The Chulalongkorn studies and the Golden Pig affair offer the police and the ministry a chance to admit that the force might have some problems. Only by recognizing the problem can they start the process of reform. But that is not the reaction we are seeing.

THE CHANG NOI CORRUPTION CURVE

3 December 1996

The Chang Noi corruption curve plots the relationship between a government's rate of graft and the length of time it stays in office. The horizontal axis plots time. The vertical axis plots the corruption rate. This rate is not an exact measure in terms of millions of baht or percentages of GDP. Rather it plots perception: how corrupt people believe the government to be. The curve illustrates a simple contemporary truth: *the more corrupt a government is, the shorter it lasts.*

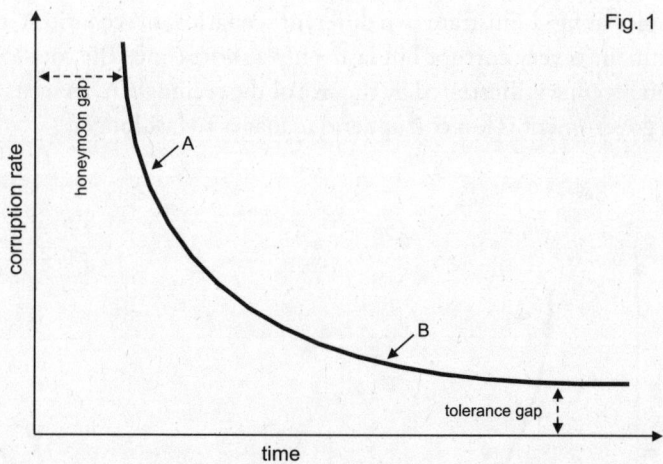

Fig. 1

The curve has a special shape with some other points of interest. At the top left, there is the *honeymoon gap*. Even if a government is amazingly corrupt, it will still have a short minimum stay in office. The public grants any new cabinet a honeymoon period. And technically it takes some time to get rid of a bad government.

At the bottom right, there is the *tolerance gap*. Society is prepared to tolerate a certain level of political corruption. Anand Panyarachun spoke last week about the need for the new cabinet to reduce corruption to a "manageable level." If a government can keep corruption below this level, then it can stay around for a long, long time.

Towards the upper left (point A), the curve rises very steeply. This shows that when a government's corruption rate rises above a certain level, public tolerance drops away rapidly, and the predicted life of the government shortens abruptly. This is the zone of public disgust.

Towards the lower right (point B), the curve drops away gently. Beyond a certain point, quite modest reductions in the rate of corruption can greatly extend a government's expected life. This is the zone of public comfort.

The size of the *total potential corruption revenue* can be calculated as the corruption rate times the length of time in office. The shaded rectangles in fig. 2 illustrate two different scenarios. In scenario A, the government is very corrupt but lasts only a short time. The total corruption revenue is illustrated by the size of the rectangle A. In scenario B, the government is less corrupt and manages to last longer.

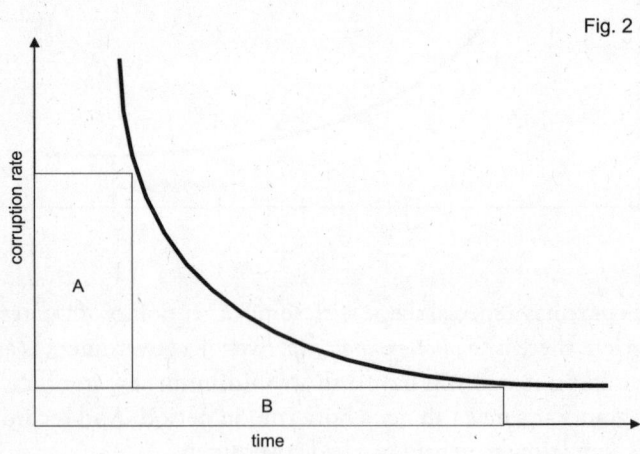

Fig. 2

Fig. 2 shows that the optimal corruption strategy depends on the relative sizes of the honeymoon gap and the tolerance gap. If a government thinks the tolerance gap is small (the people won't put up with much corruption at all) but the honeymoon gap is large (the people will always give a new government some chance), then the best strategy is to go for a high corruption rate even though it may mean only a short time in office. This is the situation illustrated in fig. 2. Rectangle A is bigger than Rectangle B. This seems to have been the strategy of the Banharn cabinet. Many ministers launched very ambitious money-making schemes in the first month in office. And the cabinet appeared to make very productive use of its final caretaker period.

For reference: both the Chatichai government (1988–91) and the Chuan government (1992–5) lasted thirty-four months, while the Banharn government (1995–6) lasted just sixteen months.

This does not mean that the Chatichai and Chuan governments had the same corruption rates. As fig. 3 shows, the curve shifts depending on the economic growth rate. If the economy is growing very fast (as during the Chatichai premiership), the curve shifts outwards. The politicians can get away with more. At a given corruption rate, they can stay in office longer.

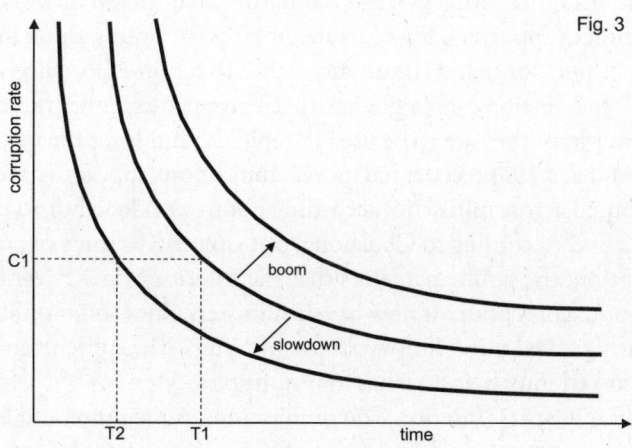

Fig. 3

More interesting right now is the opposite effect. When the growth rate drops, the curve shifts inwards. The tolerance gap shrinks: when people themselves are less well off, they are less tolerant towards political corruption. The honeymoon gap shrinks too: people look to the government for help, and will be less patient. The cabinet must reduce its corruption rate, or face being kicked out of office more quickly.

But the demand for corruption revenue tends to be rather inelastic. In other words, politicians get used to the corruption income and don't want to give it up. They also face steep inflation in the cost of running elections. Hence if a government wants to last a long time in a time of economic slowdown, it must do something positive to reduce the corruption rate.

At his press conference last week, General Chavalit was asked about the corruption issue. He replied with a saying: if the boss doesn't do it, the subordinates won't do it either. This was a clever way to draw a contrast between himself and Banharn. But Chavalit refused to commit himself to any specific anti-corruption strategy. The existing machinery for combating political corruption is notoriously defective. Chavalit appeared to say he had no plans to do anything about it. He will trust to his own good example.

A glance at the rest of his cabinet makes this seem rather optimistic. It contains more refugees from Banharn's Chat Thai than Chavalit's own direct supporters. Six of its members were among those investigated in 1991 for being "unusually rich." Two non-MPs who helped finance the election campaigns have been given posts; either these posts are rewards, or they are to be used to replenish funds for the next election. And in an unprecedented move, cabinet posts appear to have been distributed across ministries according not to workload but to potential income. According to Chulalongkorn University's study of political corruption, the public perceives that the Interior Ministry ranks top in terms of corruption. It now has six ministers. The Communications Ministry ranked third. It now has five ministers. The Agriculture Ministry ranked fourth. It now has four ministers.

Four ministries (Interior, Communications, Agriculture, and Education) account for around 60 percent of all the government budget funds for capital items and purchases of materials and equipment, which is the portion of the budget most heavily looted in the past. Between them these four now have nineteen cabinet posts.

In each of these ministries, the posts have been distributed around the various parties like candy to children. This has added a new aspect to the quota method of forming cabinets. It suggest the corruption rate could be high.

POLITICS OF SCANDAL, SCANDAL OF POLITICS

21 December 1999

The no-confidence debate has become an annual festival—a political Songkran, with dirty water poured over the nation's rulers. Such festivals seem to be the same each year. But actually they change. This year, the celebration was longer. This recognized an important fact: Chuan Two has been a great age of scandals. Let's just recall the main ones.

Salween. A senior forestry official burst into Government House with 5 million baht in an old cardboard box. He claimed the money was an attempted bribe. He could not think what else to do except give it to the PM on live TV.

The press and TV detailed how up to twenty thousand logs had been felled illegally in the Salween forests, and laundered through Burma. In a newspaper interview, the log-dealer[22] at the center of the affair made a virtual confession, boasted of his powerful connections, and showed off the diamond-studded belt holding up his jeans.

What happened? The official with the 5 million baht in a box lost his job. Six forestry officials were disciplined. The police said they were just about to file a case against the diamond-belted log dealer. That was over three months ago. Meanwhile illegal logging has been reported in at least eight other national forests.

Edible Fence.[23] The Agriculture Ministry distributed a glossy package of seeds to farmers. It made a TV ad boasting how this project would rescue rural Thailand from the economic crisis. It was leaked that the seeds were overpriced by about ten times. The ad disappeared.

---

22. Som Chankrajang, see "Chavalit and the Salween Saga," pp. 25–6.

23. The project was headlined *Phak suan khrua rua kin dai*, "Kitchen vegetables, the edible fence." Chang Noi first heard about the project in a Yasothon village where farmers showed the seed packets and dissolved in laughter at the idea the Ministry of Agriculture thought it could teach them to grow vegetables.

The deputy minister had to resign. The Counter Corruption Commission found evidence of massive collusion by lots of officials. Leaks from the probe suggested the scam went right to the top of a certain political party. The Agriculture Ministry promptly launched its own probe. Forty-seven officials were disciplined for minor "negligence." The minister declared the case closed.

Public Health. The deputy minister of health lifted price control on drugs and medical equipment. Provincial hospitals were instructed to buy supplies from specified companies at two to ten times the market price. Appalled doctors blew the whistle. Two ministers were forced to resign. The head of the ministry was suspended. The press carried detailed accounts of how the scandal had been organized. The Counter Corruption Commission ruled that there was no evidence to proceed with a criminal charge against anyone else involved, either politician or official. Subsequent probes have been similarly sandbagged.[24]

Si Nakharin. Three luxurious villas were being built on land which looked suspiciously like forest land. The documents had been issued improperly. The Accelerated Rural Development Department was building a road that happened to go to these houses and nowhere else. The scandal quickly started to snowball. Down the road another two to three thousand other plots, supposed to be resettlement for displaced local villagers, were owned by military men, Bangkok socialites, and relatives of the deputy governor. Another thousand plots were identified at Khao Laem reservoir with nice lakeside locations and boat jetties. Another 1,000 rai in Ranong were owned by those nice people from Phuket who gave us the *SPK 4-01* scandal. An enormous hilltop house in a national park in Udon was emblazoned with the personal emblem of an ex-minister. This snowball was getting too big and dangerous. Everything went totally quiet. Recent attempts to reopen the case have been sternly resisted by men in uniform.

---

24. Through extraordinary tenacity by NGOs, especially Rossana Tositrakul, in 2003 the deputy minister of health, Rakkiat Sukthana, was sentenced by the Supreme Court to fifteen years in jail for masterminding this scheme.

Rice support. Government provided money for rice millers to buy paddy at guaranteed prices. Some millers simply took the money and revalued stocks of paddy they had bought earlier at much cheaper rates. Others were so impressed by this accounting trick that it was copied all over the northeast. The bookkeeping required collusion by local officials. When the scandal broke, one of these officials fainted under questioning. Chuan said: "We will not let the guilty escape unpunished." So far no charges have been laid.

Nong Ngu Hao airport landfill. A Prime Minister's Office committee ruled that the bidding for the contract had been rigged, and the pricing vastly inflated. It suggested both politicians and officials had been involved. The contract is worth 6.8 billion baht. So far nothing has happened.

Enough. There's still computer software, flying house registrations, Samut Prakan elections, highway police, kickbacks in the port, the Food and Drug Authority, the Khurusapha textbook scandal, various banks, and a host of mini-scandals about smuggled cars, German gangsters, fake CDs, and amphetamines.

This eruption of scandals is happening because more people are prepared to act as whistle-blowers. The economic crisis has made many people less tolerant. The passage of the 1997 Constitution has fostered a hope that ordinary people can challenge the powerful. Newspapers have discovered that scandalization sells copies.

But all this whistle-blowing is not yet getting much in the way of concrete results. No living Thai politician has been seriously punished for corruption. The old Counter Corruption Commission (now superseded) never once succeeded in punishing a senior official over a major scandal.

Scandals are changing. In the past, there were two types: systematic siphoning and redistribution within bureaucratic departments; and politicians' schemes to earn one-off backhanders from contracts and other big expenditures. But recent scandals are different. Politicians and high officials work together. See the Edible Fence and Public Health scandals. Ministers make a crucial change in regulation; officials implement the systems to inflate the prices; everybody collects.

This collusion is effective. As long as the politicians and officials stick together, they can smother any scandal with investigative committees and bureaucratic delaying tactics. They can rely on the short attention span of the media.

Moreover, there is a "Chuan effect." He of course is as clean as a whistle, but he has to keep his coalition afloat. Whenever a scandal breaks, he says in his soft voice that everything will be taken care of by the law. His own halo serves as an umbrella for his less angelic colleagues.

But there are positive signs. First, the new National Counter Corruption Commission has a lot more and sharper teeth than the old one did. We have yet to see how it will use those teeth, but at least it has them.

Second, although very few big people have been legally punished over these scandals, yet some have been *publicly* punished. Three ministers were forced to resign. This had never happened before.

Third, political leaders are becoming worried. Chavalit announced he would have the police run background checks on all his party's candidates at the next election. Of course, this announcement was wonderfully ludicrous. It shows a touching faith in the police. But it does suggest a growing sensitivity.

Fourth, civic groups are not giving up. Chang Noi's person-of-the-year prize goes to Khun Rossana Tositrakul who is still resisting the repeated attempts of the politicians and officials to bury the public health scandal.

Finally, the recent no-confidence festival showed another glimmer of light. The big scandals now have party labels on them. Si Nakharin is a Democrat scandal. The Edible Fence is a Chat Thai scandal. Public Health is rapidly becoming a Democrat scandal. And so on. These scandals then become bargaining chips in the arm-wrestling between parties. Forget Si Nakharin or I'll unearth the Chat Thai connection to Rakesh Saxena. Lay off the Public Health scandal or I'll reopen the Edible Seeds case. This is blackmail and brinkmanship of a high order. And very difficult for the politicians to control.

How much longer before a political party recognizes that there could be real electoral advantage in being The Clean Party?

TWO TYPES OF CORRUPTION

5 March 2001

At the end of this parliament's first debate, prime minister Thaksin repeated his commitment to fight poverty, fight drugs, and fight corruption. It sounds great. Nobody could disagree with the sentiment. But what does he mean by "corruption"?

Corruption comes in many forms, but two are important. The first is a kind of "corruption tax" which politicians and bureaucrats collect by taking commission fees, padding expenditure budgets, and so on. This is simple theft, and very familiar.

The second type is more complex. This corruption is part of the money which politicians and their friends earn from businesses which charge high prices because they have acquired a monopoly. Let's take an example. Suppose a company acquires a license to operate a mobile phone system. Suppose there are so few such licenses that the companies conspire to charge monthly fees higher than almost anywhere else in the world. Then the company might make such high profits that its owner becomes a multi-billionaire in five years.

Economists call this sort of excess profit "rent." It's perfectly legal. But from the point of view of the average citizen, the two types of corruption are just the same. They both transfer money from our pockets into the pockets of the politicians and their business allies.

One way to view politics is simply as a contest to claim this income. Some people get together to form a political party. They pool their resources (cash, friends, connections) to campaign for election with the aim of forming a cabinet, running the country, and making money. But there is another element. Under a democratic system of government with a judicial system, corruption also has costs. The corrupt politicians might get caught, tried, fined, and jailed. They might face social derision. They might fail at the polls and lose their upfront investment.

We can express all of this as a simple formula. Suppose A is the old-fashioned commission-fee type of corruption, B is the rent from excess profits obtained by political means, and K are the costs of getting caught. The final net corruption revenue (V) can be calculated as $V = A + B - K$. Net corruption income equals commission fees plus monopoly profits less costs. Once in power, political parties will try to maximize their corruption revenue by increasing the amount of A and B, while reducing the amount of K.

How do they reduce the amount of K, the costs of corruption? These costs are high if the parliamentary opposition is strong, the judiciary is effective, the public is vigilant, and the media is independent and highly principled. So a government which wants to make corruption revenue (of either type) will do several things.

It will weaken the opposition by co-opting its most effective speakers, or digging up dirt about its past record. It will undermine the judiciary by co-opting key people into the system of corruption and revenue-sharing. It may try to subvert public vigilance by suppressing political activity. It may want to control the media, either through legal restrictions or through more subtle methods: buying controlling interests in media companies; using the advertising budgets of the government and of the corporations supporting the coalition to intimidate media owners to cooperate; bribing journalists, or just simply being so nice to them that they feel bound to reciprocate.

In other words, a corrupt government will be detrimental to a democratic system. It may also be damaging to economic growth.

If the politicians share out business monopolies among themselves (telecommunications concessions, media licenses, construction contracts), people have to pay higher prices for these things. Consumers get less for the same amount of spending. Their welfare declines. Income is redistributed to the monopoly holders. The economy may shrink because monopolies reduce output to make prices high.

But the economic effect also depends on what the businessmen-politicians do with V, the net corruption revenue. If they invest this money in business growth and innovation, then the final impact may be very positive. Indeed, the so-called "Asian model" of economic growth worked by allowing businesses to make super-profits, but then forcing them to reinvest these profits in innovation and expansion.

But in many developing countries, these super-profits don't get spent so usefully. They get ploughed back into politics, swelling the amount of money slushing around in "money politics." Or they are spent on luxurious lifestyles—buying a Porsche, drinking expensive wine, building enormous houses, presenting Daimlers to colleagues in return for favors, and so on.

Politically privileged monopolies are likely to slow down the economy, and reduce people's real income and welfare. They also create a situation in which the transition to full democracy is delayed. Reform in the judiciary gets obstructed. Attempts to liberalize the media are undermined. Elections are still flooded with money. Schemes to allow proper monitoring of highly valuable properties such as telecommunication concessions are sabotaged. Bureaucratic reform is delayed because underpaid officials are cheaper to buy. The people become frustrated and lose faith in democracy.

Does this sound familiar?

The drafters of the new constitution of 1997 tried to increase K, the costs of corruption, by making elections more difficult to buy. They also tried to reduce A (old-fashioned commission fee corruption) by strengthening the counter-corruption machinery. They did not think very much about B, the "rents" earned from politically protected business monopolies. The measures to prevent a conflict of interest between ministerial power and business benefit are not effective. They have only created some very rich wives and sons. This makes no difference in a culture where business is family based.

The government's commitment to fight corruption deserves praise and support. But corruption is changing. And many cabinet members in this government have a real conflict of interest: they are part of the problem as well as part of the solution.

A GUIDE TO MAKING MONEY ON BIG GOVERNMENT PROJECTS

27 May 2002

A decade ago, many people got worried about corruption in big government projects, particularly those involving construction. The Anand Panyarachun governments (1991–2) created a lot of new rules to control it—stricter bidding procedures, anti-collusion laws, environmental and social impact studies, and so on. But rest assured. If you have the right political contacts, some seed capital, and a burning desire to make lots and lots of money, it's still possible. Here is a simple, step-by-step user's guide.

1. Install your man in the key decision-making role in the relevant ministry. Usually the best post is the department head. With luck, the position is available at a price payable to the minister overseeing the appointment. You can raise the money by clubbing together with like-minded colleagues who have interests in other big projects. In some sophisticated ministries, the payment can be made as a deposit upfront, followed by installments depending on the success in generating returns.

2. Create or activate some suitably grandiose project. Make sure it is planned on a turnkey basis. This is critical because it allows much more flexibility at the later stages.

3. Find a friend with a consultancy company. Or just set one up with your friends. You might want to have a share in the company in order to exert some control, but you should keep this hidden. Companies based overseas or at least headed by foreigners look very good in this role, and are often good performers. One such consultancy company once offered to make Chang Noi "very rich" for just endorsing a report. Expertise is not a problem. There is a good supply of underpaid academics, both here and overseas. Ensure this company is engaged to write the specification for the project.

4. At the bidding stage, make sure all serious competitors are somehow removed. There used to be a very good system for doing this, known as *hua*, which shared major projects around a select syndicate of contractors. But then the government passed an anti-collusion law. Luckily the law was written in such a way that the procedures laid down are far too complex. It's simply unworkable and hence is usually ignored. Some people think this was a very clever piece of law drafting.

5. Set up a state enterprise to oversee the project. By doing this, you can avoid many of the strict rules which government departments have to follow when they manage such projects.

6. Forget to do the environmental impact study or social impact study, even if it is technically required by the rules. By the time NGOs find out about the project, and people affected by it start to protest, you should have the foundations finished. It will be too late.

7. Once the contractor is chosen, revise the project and increase the budget. This is the beauty of the turnkey format. You can present the revisions as technically superior, or of greater public benefit, or whatever. You can even change the location if a friend has a piece of land on which he would like to make a nice profit. These changes have to go through the cabinet, but usually this does not seem to be a problem.

8. Set up other companies to act as subcontractors. They can do things like buying the land for the project, or supplying materials. Luckily the rules on conflict-of-interest are so poor that you can subcontract to a company in which many of those directly involved—ministers, officials—have a share. These days, however, journalists and NGOs are sometimes too inquisitive. Unless you are a really "big" name, it's probably best not to have your name on the company registration. Instead, you can hold *hun lom*, "wind shares," which are as invisible as the wind. This is one of those techniques which, like putting shares in the name of your cook and gardener, seems to be alright because "everybody does it."

9. Once you have the system set up, you must keep using it. Your first effort might have resulted in a project which is obviously overpriced, perhaps even useless, and very destructive for natural resources and local communities. But don't get too upset. Thailand is full of underused

wastewater and rubbish incinerator schemes, oddly wide stretches of road, and dams which don't seem to work. For future projects, you can even increase the profit by reusing an old project design in a new location, even if it was a bit of a disaster first time round.

You might think this guide is too ambitious—that controls could not be so lax, and the money-making opportunities could not be so big and easy. Not so. A team from Chulalongkorn University is just completing a study of contract and procurement practices in some recent big projects like the Khlong Dan wastewater facility, Suvarnabhumi airport at Nong Ngu Hao, and the Bang Pakong dam. The study shows that all of this is common practice. It reckons you should be able to get away with 10 to 20 percent of the budget. Add in the normal business profit and that could rise to 30 or 40 percent.

The Chula study also shows that the procedures for designing, allocating, and monitoring projects in Thailand are much looser than in countries like Hong Kong, Germany, and Denmark. Loopholes everywhere. These other countries have systems to screen questionable contractors out of the bidding process. They have bidding procedures which are workable and transparent. They have an expert agency to oversee the bidding process. They have conflict-of-interest rules which prevent officials and politicians having an interest in a company which acts as a contractor or subcontractor.

There are rumors that the WTO will force Thailand to tighten things up. Maybe. In the meantime, happy contracting!

TALES FROM THE SWAMP

13 June 2005

Khunying Jaruvarn Maintaka[25] has said almost every procurement contract for the new airport is problematic. For fifty years, the tales emerging from this swamp have been about authoritarian rule and funny deals.

Almost half a century ago, American advisers suggested the Thai government should have a new commercial airport. The military dictator Sarit Thanarat decided it should be located in Nong Ngu Hao, Cobra Swamp. Nobody seems to know why Sarit made this choice. There was no study of the site's suitability, no consideration of alternatives. The choice set off a minor orgy of land speculation.

One company, Italthai Holdings, was given the contract to build the airport. There was no competitive bidding. The same company would research, design, and manage the construction. Critics thought this was a license to print money. The controversy became so heated that when Sarit died in 1963, the project immediately fell apart.

But great ideas don't die easily. Sarit's successors kept trying to kick-start it, and finally succeeded in 1968. Again they selected a company without competitive bidding, the US aviation giant, Northrop. Again

---

25. Jaruvarn Maintaka was appointed auditor-general in 2001 after a career as an auditor in public service. In 2003, the Constitutional Court ruled that her appointment had been procedurally incorrect and was therefore invalid. It was widely believed that she had been over zealous in investigations into spending by the Thaksin government, especially for the new Bangkok airport. She refused to resign on grounds, "I came to take the position as commanded by a royal decision, so I will leave the post only when directed by such a decision." When the Senate nominated a replacement for her, the king did not give the royal assent. In February 2006, she was reinstated. After the 2006 coup, she became a member of the Assets Examination Committee, which prepared several corruption cases against Thaksin and froze almost 2 billion baht belonging to Thaksin and family in Thai banks on grounds it had been corruptly acquired.

they commissioned the company both to design and construct the air-port, and threw in a concession to operate it for twenty years as well. Again Italthai (renamed as Italian-Thai) popped up as Northrop's local partner.

Again, too, controversy surged. The press argued it was a ramp. Parliament rejected the project three times. The deal was finalized only after the military strongmen abolished parliament and went back to dictatorial rule in 1971.

And again it fell apart when dictatorial rule was brought down by the student revolt of 1973. The successor government walked away from the deal. For good measure, Northrop's banker was accused of improperly financing Nixon's presidential reelection campaign, and Northrop had to pull out of the deal.

But when military rule returned in the late 1970s, so too did the airport in Cobra Swamp. By 1984 there was a master plan. But there was also an oil crisis and a big budget deficit, so the project was put on ice.

When generals returned to power by coup in 1991, the project finally took off. But times had changed. The generals could no longer pick a site and a company at will. The process now involved four main parties, each of which was wreathed in controversy.

First, control of the project was relocated to an independent authority. This idea was conceived in 1991–2, and finally evolved into the New Bangkok International Airport company (NBIA) in 1995–6. Although this put some distance between the project and the politicians, it was not much of a gap. There was a battle royal between the air force and the civilian ministers of Anand Panyarachun's government over who would appoint and control the authority's members. From then on, almost every change of cabinet (and even some reshuffles) was promptly followed by a total revision of the key positions.

Second, design work was allocated to strings of consultant companies. How they wrote the specs was often critical in determining which companies would get the resulting contracts. Although the basic design was made in the early 1990s, each successive government found reasons to adjust the project so that a new set of consultants could be appointed, and a new set of specs written. Under Chuan I, the project was re-imagined as a hub for the Southeast Asian region. Under Chuan II, grandiose plans were scaled back because of the economic crisis. Under Thaksin, the project was reconceived as bigger than ever.

Third, construction and supply contracts were now allocated by competitive bidding, but often this process was cleverly managed. A ring of major contractors was suspected of sharing out contracts; they formed a queue, predetermined who would win, and compensated one another through subcontracts. But sometimes this could go wrong.

One big contract for landfill was won by Italian-Thai. Thirteen other companies complained they had been disqualified from the bidding because of the way the specs had been written. The associations of architects and engineers estimated the padding in the 11.6 billion baht price was a cool 3.5 billion. The aggrieved companies petitioned the Ministry of Communications, the Counter Corruption Commission, and the Council of State.

Eventually the Council of State ruled that the bidding had been improper. But Italthai kept the contract, which by that time was far advanced. Only the scale and cost were renegotiated in the downsizing dictated by the economic crisis.

Fourth, financiers also had influence. The major battle over the last decade has been about the design and construction of the passenger terminal, for which one major financier was the Japan Bank for International Cooperation (JBIC). At one bidding round, the five consortiums with no Japanese member all withdrew, leaving the four with a Japanese member to fight it out.

But this was a mere skirmish. The struggle over the terminal building was a major war in which all four elements of this new era were in play. By a tortuous process, two designs were made, and each was backed by its own coalition of politicians, executives in NBIA, consultant companies, contractors, and financiers. The battle raged back and forth for years amid a blizzard of corruption charges and counter-charges. Eventually, the contract went to ITO, a consortium in which the major partner is Italian-Thai. This decision was promptly challenged on grounds that the specs had been biased, the process had skipped several important steps, the scrutiny was inadequate, and Italian-Thai should be disqualified because it was in the bankruptcy court. Most of all, the contract seemed full of loopholes, including provisions to reduce the scope of work without reducing the cost.

What kept the project moving was the factor which has marked every significant stage in its long history: a revival of authoritarian rule. The decline of media freedom, and the general decay of public and institutional scrutiny under Thaksin, made scandal disappear from sight—but, of course, not from the real world.

HOW TO BUY A COUNTRY

31 July 2000

Many of you would like to have a country. To realize this ambition in the past, you needed a good family name and a big army. But times have changed. Today we live in the age of markets. All you need is money. The technique is still a bit tricky. But if you follow this easy 10-point guide, you should be able to purchase a country.

1. Get a monopoly. A handful is even better. In the past, you could generate the necessary funds by mere crime—smuggling oil, stripping forests, running drugs, hosting illegal gambling. That's still fine if your ambitions run no higher than your own province or a part-share in the Ministry of Interior. But to secure a country, you need the spectacular profit levels of monopolies.

2. Wait for a crisis. A full-strength financial disaster will lower the price level and take most of your competitors out of the market. You might want to bring in the IMF as a strategic partner because they're really the experts on making these as bad as possible. You just have to make sure that your investment funds get less damaged than everybody else's. So get access to the necessary insider information.

3. Recruit an appealing start-up team. This should be very broadly based, with something to appeal to everyone. Two bankers. A couple of ex-finance ministers. A few professors. A general or two. A handful of idealists. This is not difficult as there are lots of these people around and many are endearingly naive and easily flattered. Don't worry about the long term. Most of them will fade away when things get more serious.

4. Get a marketing team. Ideally the key people should have experience in marketing political products in the past. Don't worry that your product is very different to what they have handled before (sometimes this is called "ideology"). These marketeers get bored easily. They like the challenge of handling something that is new. If you're rather pasty

looking and a boring speaker, that only increases the challenge and makes them more creative and hard-working.

5. Put up pictures of yourself in every available space throughout the country. Heads of state have traditionally smothered countries with their image *after* acquiring power. Now it's a way of establishing prior right of ownership. Of course all this clutter messes up the natural environment. And you may be embarrassed at seeing yourself everywhere frozen in some fatuous pose. But remember, this is politics in the age of markets. This strategy works for laundry detergent, fizzy drinks, and female underwear. It'll work for you.

6. Buy every politician that's not nailed down. This is where point 2 (waiting for a crisis) really starts to pay off. Many will be hard-up or deeply in debt. Many will be rightly worried about their own personal safety if they fail to keep up the usual payments to their armies of hangers-on. It helps too if it has been a long time since the last election. The future will be more unpredictable. Many politicians will be feeling very insecure. But you must never buy politicians with a one-off payment. Installment systems are much safer and more effective. And keep the big installments to the end. These so-called "fertilizer formulas,"[26] like 2-3-5-15-15, are much misunderstood. The big figures are not very serious and you don't need to include them in your cost projections. Most politicians are gamblers. They are mesmerized by the idea of "the big one," the jackpot. You can exploit this by offering something that is always "over the rainbow."

7. Promise, promise, promise. Cash is not the only currency you have for buying up politicians. Some can be bought by the promise of good jobs which offer status, indemnity, and revenue opportunities. You may actually have rather few of such good jobs to offer. But don't worry. They're recyclable. You can offer each job to many different people. Of course these rivals will find out about this because

---

26. These formulas were supposed to show the amounts, in million baht, which the candidate would receive at various stages of the campaign—on making the deal; on starting campaigning; on getting elected; etc. The name derives from the formulas used to show the combination of chemicals in fertilizer.

people like to boast and the press loves stirring up this sort of thing. But history has shown this is manageable. These rivals won't start open warfare before the election because they don't want to screw up even a fractional chance. And after the polls, the scrapping will look messy but won't matter a bit.

8. Buy a bank and a TV station. Close to the polls, when cash management becomes critical, banks become really useful. In the past you could rely on strategic partnerships for this service. But lately politicians have not done a good job of looking after the bankers, so you might need a strategic stake to make sure of things. Television stations are only just coming onto the market, and their utility is a bit unknown. But simply as a block on your rivals, buy a bit of any that become available.

9. Don't touch the money. The former Japanese premier, Tanaka, liked to keep big bundles of yen stacked in his house and handed them out like bricks. This method is ideal because politicians are always seduced by the look, smell, and feel of real money. But in these days of election commissions and anti-corruption bodies, this technique has become too risky. Use electronic transfers, preferably offshore, and have a staff to handle them (wives are useful, here). Then you can always face the press, put on your most angelic face, say something like "I have never bought anyone," and still return in your next life as something no worse than a toad.

10. Repeat endlessly the well-known formula: "I have never used money to buy politicians and votes. My opponents accuse me of such things because it is what they do themselves." Nobody will notice the circular logic. People expect to hear you say this, so don't let them down.

HOW TO SELL A COUNTRY

11 February 2006

At the end of 2000, just before Thaksin came to power, the market value of Shin Corp was 46.1 billion baht. The Shinawatra-Dhamaphong families and their sundry household staff probably owned about half— say 23 billion. This stake has just been sold for 73.3 billion. It roughly tripled over five years, a rate of growth of 26 percent. Not bad when the economy is growing around 5 percent. All boats rise, but some rise a lot more than others.

Of course, you would like to do as well. Here is an easy guide.

1. Before you can sell a country, you first have to acquire one. Business is fine, but the rate-of-return improves magnificently when business is combined with political power. It's usually quite difficult to buy a country on the open market, but after a devastating financial crisis the price weakens and most competitors are taken out of the picture (see the previous article).

2. Acquire politicians. The price is surprisingly reasonable. Buying in job-lots is more efficient (sometimes called party mergers), but the basic principle is to acquire any that are not nailed down. Your target should be to acquire the number needed to ensure the parliament cannot submit you to any serious scrutiny.

3. Have a core business in which the profit level is ultimately determined by government rules rather than market competition. A licensed casino monopoly would be perfect, but a good second-best is a near-monopoly business operating under a government concession with a built-in advantage over competitors. Then all you have to do is to keep the existing arrangements in place. Sabotage the regulatory environment. Delay calls for market liberalization. Even improve your own concession terms if you're feeling ambitious. Competitors will wear themselves out complaining about playing fields not being level, while you maintain your market share and profit level.

4. Diversify into areas where governmental actions can again have a significant impact on returns. Tax holidays under investment promotion rules or cheap finance from public-sector banks are good. Best is to buy a business which is unprofitable because of a strict government licensing agreement and high concession fees. Then simply tearing up the agreement and lowering the concession fee will have a spectacular effect on profits. It's also a good idea to diversify into areas where you know government policies should improve the prospects, such as air travel or health care or personal finance. And work on that idea of a casino monopoly in the future.

5. Stamp hard on any possible sources of scrutiny or criticism. Buy up any TV stations on the market. Reverse any trend towards liberalization in electronic media under state control. Whip the press into line by threatening their bottom lines. Get friends to buy stakes in newspapers that still don't understand. Close down any production companies, radio stations, websites, or satellite TV channels that utter a squeak of criticism. Put friends in all regulatory and oversight bodies. Harass NGOs. Ridicule intellectuals. Intimidate everybody with a lethal anti-drug campaign. Strew the country with defamation suits. Pour scorn on democracy, rights, and the rule of law.

6. Be absolutely clear about what you're doing. Say things like: "As a prime minister, my motto is: You must be rich and don't stop becoming richer!"

7. Get the most respectable bank in the country to finance and otherwise assist some of the most flagrant deals. This makes things look a little bit better all round. Banks generally have no conscience so this is quite easy to organize.

8. Sell while you are still in power. This is vital. Your family companies are worth a lot more when investors believe you have the power to improve their profits. Sell to another country where business and politics are delicately intertwined, and potential criticism is kept well under control. This will maximize mutual understanding. Shortly before the sale, engineer a few changes in laws and regulations which raise the attractiveness to the buyer. Only you are in a position to do such things, so don't be shy. Choose the sale method which minimizes the

tax liability. In the process you might have to break several other laws and rules such as disclosure obligations, foreign shareholding limits, or whatever. Don't worry about these because the penalties are minor and anyway you are the boss of the people who impose those penalties. Tax laws can change with the seasons. Precedents are meaningless. Make sure all the relevant regulatory bodies and government departments are ready to mount a smokescreen. Officials don't need to know any details. Just keep on saying: the prime minister can do no wrong. Don't get sentimental about how these people might be feeling inside. Conscience is a luxury. This is about money. Have a team of Dobermans on the government payroll to snarl and snap at any critics.

9. Take no notice of the international reaction. The foreign press will start to portray your country just like a banana republic run by some murderous kleptomaniac. Ignore it. Forget that you have constantly accused your own critics of damaging the country's image. Forget that you came to power by sledging your opponents for selling the country. As you own the country, nationalism is whatever helps you.

10. There is one regulatory body not under your control. The big one. There's some risk you could come back as a flea, or even get stranded in the Lokanta depths.[27] Try bargaining. Promise to give away all your property several times over in your next life. This is only a bit more outrageous than what you promise the people at election times. It might work.

---

27. Those who have harmed their parents, monks, or Brahmin teachers are reborn in the Lokanta hell, the lowest hell in the Three Worlds cosmology. It exists in the gap between universes, and hence is totally devoid of any light. Each person there cannot see the others and believes himself the sole inhabitant.

WHO PAYS FOR POLITICS?

15 May 2006

Last week, Khunying Pojaman Shinawatra was reported telling a Thai Rak Thai (TRT) Party meeting that she would bear only half the costs of the coming election. She called on other leaders to chip in. How much do they need? And where does the money come from?

Matichon recently (7 May) calculated that the average cost per constituency at the 2005 election was 20 million baht, shared half-half between the candidate and the party. That would make the TRT Party's share about 4 billion baht for the whole country.

Besides these campaign costs, the party also needs a regular budget. Most TRT MPs are said to receive a regular monthly retainer from the party or their faction head. One senator recently said that some seventy to eighty of the previous senators were also on the payroll. These payments have been estimated as high as 200,000 baht per head per month, but *Matichon* plumped for a more conservative estimate of 50,000. On top there are large publicity costs. Political leaders and political parties no longer advertise themselves only at campaign times, but keep up a constant drip-feed of ads, just like detergent brands. Then there are the running costs of TRT's splendid big building. With sundries, this must all add up to 2 to 3 billion baht a year.

TRT's exceptional presence in Thai politics over the past six years has been underwritten by exceptional amounts of cash. Where does this come from? Since the party's foundation, Khunying Pojaman has been the largest donor according to the official figures. But her generous largesse nowhere near covers the estimated budget for the party's running expenses and election campaign costs. Other leaders of this billionaires' party have chipped in. In 2005, party-list candidacies and ministerships were awarded to some big moneybags, including alleged stock market fraudsters. Still, it's difficult to account fully for TRT's massive financial power in Thai politics.

Recently a suggestion appeared in the fourth of the series of *Ru than thaksin* (Understanding Thaksin) books edited by former senator, Chirmsak Pinthong. This volume is subtitled "The Insiders," though "The Rat Laundry" might have been more appropriate. Four former supporters of Thaksin explain why they have defected (ratted), and try to justify (launder) their past actions in supporting him.

The longest confession is from Snoh Thienthong, who truly qualifies as an "insider." He was formerly adviser, whip, and deputy leader of the TRT Party, and number 18 on the TRT party list in both 2001 and 2005. He connived with Thaksin in the infamous land deal over the Alpine golf course, and has often claimed to be the kingmaker who put Thaksin into power.

In this book, Snoh makes the following allegation.

"He placed one of his own people in every ministry. These people did not need to have a powerful post, but everybody knew who they were ... If any minister wanted to propose a project using the central budget, the minister would first have to clear it with 'his person' first. Many ministers were approached by 'his person' saying, 'The budget is coming. You can have 5 or 6 billion, but 10 percent must go to the party ... Any minister who would not do this, could not remain."

Snoh then explained how the system worked.

"For this 10 percent policy, the minister would have to pad the budget proposed for approval to include the 10 percent that would go to the party. Then once it was agreed with 'his person' via Khunying, the matter could be sent to his trusted 'permanent political representative,' who used to be his company employee. To date nobody knows how much this ten percent amounts to. Probably need to ask Khunying."

Snoh claims to have asked Khunying what she needed so many billions for, and got this answer: "In politics you have to hand out money. It has to be considered a business." Snoh asked her what would happen if things blew up, and she replied, "If Thaksin falls, the Thai Rak Thai Party will have to stay in power for at least two more terms for safety."

Of course, allegations over percentage commissions on budget projects are nothing new at all. It is other aspects of this allegation which make it so arresting.

First, the centralization. We are used to hearing about gangs of ministers, senior officials, and businessmen conspiring to take a percentage on budget projects through overpricing and similar devices. But this allegation suggests another subtraction which supplants or (more likely) supplements that form of corruption. We are told there is a centrally directed network that reaches into "every ministry." Ten percent of the total capital budget is around 20 billion baht.

Second, the proceeds are alleged to be channeled to the TRT Party. In other words, Snoh alleges that the party's massive financial strength is financed by the taxpayer.

Is Snoh credible? He's a very old-style politician. He gave Thaksin considerable help and has a lot to excuse himself for. He has been gradually sidelined by Thaksin over the last five years, and has reasons for feeling aggrieved. He still has political ambitions and has already launched his own new party. His allegation could be seen as nothing more than another move in the political chess game.

But that makes it all the more extraordinary that the accusation has brought forth no pained denial, no counter-charge, and none of the defamation suits which have become the confetti of Thai politics. This allegation was not some careless statement heard by a few people. It was not one of those newspaper reports which the speaker can deny on the following day and blame on journalistic incompetence. It appeared in print in a signed article in a book which has become quickly very popular. Is there silence because Snoh is so lacking in credibility that denial is deemed unnecessary? Or is he too close to the truth for comfort?[28]

---

28. Snoh Thienthong quit TRT in 2006, and said several other damaging things about Thaksin. The rift seemed total. After the December 2007 election, Snoh immediately aligned his Pracharaj Party with PPP, the reincarnation of TRT. Snoh's wife became a minister in the Samak government engineered by Thaksin from exile. According to rumors, this touching reconciliation cost 700 million baht.

Water and trees

KAENG SUA TEN: BIG DAM ISSUE

10 December 1996

Why has the Kaeng Sua Ten dam project become such an emotive issue?

Partly it's because of the complexity of the interests involved. Local: Sa-iab villagers want to protect their homes and livelihood. Regional: residents of the Yom valley believe the dam will give them irrigation, flood control, and electricity. National: environmentalists defend the Mae Yom forests as unique and irreplaceable national assets.

More importantly, it's because Kaeng Sua Ten is not one battle but three, and because all three touch on larger issues. At the core, Kaeng Sua Ten is part of the long-running battle between city and locality over the control of resources. On top, Kaeng Sua Ten has become a focus for conflict between officials and environmentalists over the meaning of "development." And more recently, Kaeng Sua Ten is at the center of the struggle between established authority and popular participation. For all involved, Kaeng Sua Ten is no longer just a dam, but a symbol, an issue, a cause.

City vs. locality. Along with golf courses, waste disposal plants, and eucalyptus plantations, dams are the flashpoints of the city-locality battle over resources.

For the city, dams bring benefits of electricity, water supply, flood control, and opportunities for profit from logging and construction. For the locality, dams mean displacement of people, destruction of the forest, and disruption of fish stocks.

Beyond this simple profit-loss account, dams have become powerful visual symbols of the resource battle. Every brochure on "development" has a shot of a large hydro-dam, angled to stress its sheer size, its clean swooping lines, its massed energy. But in the locality, dams are a visual intrusion. Their dull grayness violates the green-brown tones of the forest. Their sleek mass contrasts with the fine detail of nature. Their enormity disrupts the scale of the environment.

Officials vs. environmentalists. In the 1960s and 1970s, dam building was one of the major crusades of official-led development. Then the environmentalists pointed out that Thailand had lost half of its forests in a generation, partly through dam building. They joined with villagers to oppose the Nam Choan dam project, which would destroy a large chunk of the largest remaining forest in mainland Southeast Asia. In a long acrimonious battle, the project was shelved in 1982, revived in 1986, and then abandoned completely in 1988. In the wake of this victory, the environmental lobby managed to block four other hydro-dam projects.

The authorities changed strategy. They abandoned projects for building big hydro-dams that would flood tracts of beautiful forest. They concentrated on smaller projects, located in less scenic and sensitive areas, with irrigation benefits for local people. The most important was the Pak Mun dam, sited where the main river system of the northeast flows into the Mekong. The authorities claimed it was a "run-of-the-river" dam which would not flood the forest, disrupt the river flow, or force many people to relocate.

Still there was a long and bitter battle. The environmental lobby complained that it was nonsense to label such a large structure as "run-of-the-river"; that the whole northeast river system would be affected; and that fish would never negotiate the dam's fish ladder because "Thai fish cannot jump." But the authorities dismissed these environmental concerns. And the authorities won. Fish attracted less popular emotional support than forests. The dam was completed in 1994.

This evened the score to one-all, with the authorities on strike. In triumph, the electricity authority vaunted the "success" of the Pak Mun project and its notorious fish ladder in press and TV advertising. The Irrigation Department launched several new projects in the northeast. Since the Nam Choan debacle, the authorities had been nervous about proposing projects which would flood forest and destroy trees. But the Pak Mun victory gave them new confidence. They revived four shelved projects in the north. One of these was Kaeng Sua Ten.

The Kaeng Sua Ten dam was first planned in 1982 as a hydro-power project. After the Nam Choan affair, it was reborn as an irrigation scheme. During the Pak Mun struggle, the project lay on the shelf. When Bangkok and much of the country was flooded in the rainy season of 1995, supporters of the project claimed it was really a flood-control scheme. When large areas of the north and central regions were again flooded in 1996, this argument surfaced again.

In fact, Kaeng Sua Ten remains an irrigation dam with the option to include some hydropower generation. If built, it will probably contribute power and water supply to new industrial areas in Phrae, as well as providing irrigation water down the Yom valley in Phichit, Phitsanulok, and Nakhon Sawan. But this constant redefinition of the dam's purpose has raised doubts. Do the authorities want to build a dam, or win another victory?

Authority vs. participation. The scale of the conflict escalated at the start of the Banharn government. Several ministers swung their weight behind the dam project. And the combination of officials and ministers tried to steamroller all doubts and queries about the project.

Agriculture minister Montri Pongpanit, science minister Yingphan Manasikarn, and deputy PM Samak Sundaravej loudly backed the project. Motives were mixed and complex. Yingphan wanted the political kudos of godfathering a project which would bring irrigation benefits to his own constituency. Several other MPs in Samak's party came from the irrigation zone. Montri's interests were less clear. The logging value of the timber was estimated at 2 billion baht.

Like the official authorities, these politicians seemed over-ardent to have the dam built. Montri brazenly announced that the golden teak forest, which opponents claimed would be destroyed by the project, simply did not exist. Environmental journalists rushed up to Phrae to take photographs showing that Montri was lying. When NGOs demanded a public hearing, Samak opposed the idea on grounds that the dam "would never be built" if people were allowed to express their views. Yingphan called meetings in the downstream area, told the attendees that the dam would save them from flooding, and claimed the subsequent show of support was a "public hearing." When even the World Bank stalled its funding because the environmental impact study was inadequate, Yingphan set up a committee staffed by the same "experts" who had made the rejected study. Army TV Channel Five made a two-part documentary on the controversy, aired the portion in support of the project, and suppressed the second part which detailed the downside.

The revival of the issue in recent weeks shows the same desire to railroad the project, and the same impatience with opposition. Banharn unblocked the project in the very dying days of his government. Official supporters are dismissive about the need for environmental studies. Samak called the project's opponents "barbarians."

But the opposition to the dam has some added strengths. Local organizations have better information and support networks than in the past. From the experience of Pak Mun and other projects, they know that official promises of compensation need to be treated with caution. They get support from the Assembly of the Poor and the network of local organizations that have emerged in recent years. They are discussing using passive resistance techniques that have proved effective in other local protests.

The environment lobby has also learned from the failure of the Pak Mun protest. It is building its campaign around a simple issue that symbolizes the arguments about sustainable development. The golden teak forest is old, extensive, and priceless as a natural laboratory of biodiversity. Why destroy something which is totally unique and irreplaceable?

The attempt to railroad the project is creating its own opposition within officialdom, among groups which question the top-down steamroller approach. The Forestry Department sponsored an environmental study which challenges the bona fides of those supporting the project. The National Parks Department is grumbling about the decision to site the dam in one of its sanctuaries. The Ministry of Interior's Damrong Rajanubhap Institute has accused irrigation officials of doctoring information about the dam. The Office of Environmental Policy and Planning and the National Environment Board have both opposed the dam and the attempts to ignore the 1992 Environment Act.

Kaeng Sua Ten is not such a big dam. But it is a very big issue. The proposed dam is located near a geological fault line. It also lies right across three major fault-lines in society, politics, and economy—locality against city, cost-benefit against sustainable development, top-down authoritarianism against participation. If it involved a simple tradeoff between a certain volume of golden teak and a certain volume of irrigation and flood control, then the resolution would just involve a choice. But Kaeng Sua Ten is more difficult than that because it raises big issues about what sort of future society we want to build: equitable, sustainable, and participatory. Or urban-biased, short-term, and authoritarian.

IN A FREE STATE

27 January 1999

We cross the border without difficulty. The frontier post is a rough wooden gate hinged by an old truck tire. Nobody asks for passports. The only guard is a proud but exhausted bitch surrounded by five scraggy new puppies.

When the villagers fenced off the village, the provincial authorities claimed they had declared a "free state." But the fence is a few rails of bamboo. Chickens, dogs, and children pass through without noticing it exists. The villagers are rather amused by the accusation. "Welcome to the free state," they beam.

The core population of the two villages in the free state are Chao Bon, a Mon-Khmer minority. They have probably been in this area longer than any Thai. They like lonely places. Gradually they have been pushed farther into the forest. A generation ago they would run away at the site of a stranger. Now many other northeasterners have joined them and intermarried. They live by collecting *bai lan*, the palm fiber on which all Siam's religious texts, chronicles, and histories were once written. Now it is used for wrapping traditional savories. Almost all the nation's supply comes from this Pa Nayang Klak forest in lower Chaiyaphum. The villagers look after the forest because it is their livelihood. They feed us a lunch of red ants' eggs, spicy mushroom, *pak wan*, and fresh vegetables. "It all comes from our pollution-free supermarket."

This "free state" seems to belong to a different century, a different Thailand. But here and now, the outside world is hammering on the door. These two villages stand in the way of the construction of the Phong Khun Phet (PKP) dam.

A lot of people believe the PKP dam will make them happier. This is a region of rain shadow. The annual rainfall is small and unreliable. Last year El Nino made things bad. This year may be worse.

Many are pinning their hopes on the PKP dam. But who will really benefit? The villagers who blocked the road on 5 January in support of the dam came mostly from the area to the north. Their hope is understandable because their area is really parched. But it is on a hill, above the planned reservoir. Nowhere in the project document is there any provision for pumping water uphill. The villagers in the area just below the dam have plenty of water in the rainy season but think the dam will help their second crop. But the project plan makes it clear that the benefits will come in the rainy season, not the dry. This plan targets the benefits to areas 100 kilometers down the Chi River in Khon Kaen. The man in charge of a pumping station some 20 kilometers down the Chi is amazed by this news; "It will never get that far."

Even so, someone will benefit. But is the PKP dam the best plan for this area? The dam will hold 70 million cubic meters of water. But the upper Chi as a whole carries 2400 million. Will anyone notice this little addition? Would it make more sense to manage the 2400 better rather than bothering with another 70?

Probably so. But managing the 2400 is a problem. Water is a very free business. Along this short stretch of the upper Chi, there are pumping stations built by the Irrigation Department, Science Ministry, and local communities. Most have no gauges. Nobody has a clear idea where, when, and how much water is pumped out. The stretch also has several weirs built by local communities. The overall layout owes much more to local initiative than any overall plan. At a newly built Science Ministry pump, the local overseer knows how to operate the on-off switch but little else. Will the flow be enough? "Don't know yet, this is the first year." What will you do if different villages fight over the supply? "No idea."

The district officer admits he used to have no interest in the PKP dam, even though the project has been discussed for over a decade. Until last year. Then the water ran out in the dry season. He had to decide which villages would get the dwindling supply. He nearly got torn apart in the process. That experience made him interested in the PKP project. His conception of how the dam will help the water system in his area bears no relationship to the project plan (which he has never read). But he has joined the legion of hope. And like any convert, his support is especially fervent. "Those villages must be removed. That forest is not worth saving anyway."

Certainly Pa Nayang Klak does not look like the lush rainforest of the picture postcards. It's dry deciduous, and outside the rainy season it looks sparse and parched. But this is the type of forest which once covered much of the northeast, and whose rapid disappearance over the last generation make the statistics of forest destruction so dramatic. The villagers in the "free state" are not the only ones who use this forest's resources. All over the northeast there are people who used to have a forest like this close at hand, and they still miss its benefits. Every now and then they get together, pile into a pickup, and head for Chaiya-phum. Some collect *bai lan*. More gather up red ants' eggs, *pak wan*, bamboo shoots, herbs, mushrooms, and the tree frogs, which can be knocked off the branches after a good storm.

These benefits don't figure in the cost-benefit analysis of the dam. Of course, not all the forest will be flooded. But the removal of a significant amount will set off a chain reaction. All the demand for *bai lan*, mushroom, red ants' eggs, and tree frogs will be concentrated in the remaining part. At some point, this pressure will pass a critical point and the forest will disappear. This has been the pattern all over the region.

The PKP project has many supporters. The Irrigation Department has already spent over 50 million baht on plans, land purchase, and compensation. The contractor has his machinery standing by idle. The land speculators are eager to cash in their profits. Many farmers (far more than can realistically benefit) have invested this dam with their own hopes. Local officials pray it will make their life easier. In a free democratic state, support in such numbers certainly matters. But is the PKP project happening because the Irrigation Department likes building dams and is no good at water management? Because it has no interest in finding more rational ways to manage the upper Chi. Because no attempt has been made to assess the real social and economic value of the forest which will be destroyed. Because too many people have been seduced by lies and bad data. Because projects acquire a momentum which is difficult to defy. Because logic gets sacrificed to emotion. Because in a free, democratic state, taking decisions which respect the past, present, and future requires a lot of effort.

MYTHS AND REALITIES OF RESETTLEMENT

15 March 1999

The valley could serve as a model for the self-reliance and mixed farming advocated by the king. Oil palms interplanted with coconut. Young rubber trees rising out of fields of pineapple. Orchards of durian and pomelo. Lines of betel palms ("we export the nuts to India"). Hillsides of banana, longan, jackfruit, mangosteen, rambutan. Even on the verge of the dry season, the lushness overwhelms. "Some prices are always up and some down. But with this variety, we are always secure."

The community, too, could be a model. There is no sign of the hollowing out caused by out-migration of the young. Has the crisis forced people to return to the village? None left in the first place. What about *ya ba* (methamphetamines)? No problem here. Over a thousand kids go down the hill each morning to the secondary school. "With this secure income, I can send my children to school and have some money left to help society."

There is just one big flaw in this pretty picture. The Irrigation Department wants to put this valley several meters under water.

In 1989, Typhoon Gay devastated Chumphon. Since then, the Irrigation Department has been planning ways to protect the low-lying town from flooding. In most years, there are floods for a few days. And when a typhoon veers in this direction, the flood is deeper and longer. Part of the scheme is to build the Rap-ror dam further up the valley to hold back the rainwater which falls on the hills and funnels down the valley slopes towards the town.

The villagers in the valley were also hit by Typhoon Gay. Houses were smashed, trees flattened. They have rebuilt this model of mixed farming over the subsequent decade, and they are rightly proud of it. They were poor for many years while the valley revived. Their houses are still small and simple. The *wat* has a roof but no walls and only an earth floor. But now they are comfortable. The oil palms deliver a monthly income as steady as a government salary. Most families have a pickup truck. A few more years and they will be well off. "We don't want to have to start again. We don't want our community broken up. We don't want to be sent to a rocky nowhere and have no money to send our kids to school."

The dam scheme plans to move them to a nearby valley. The map shows an empty area divided up into a neat grid of resettlement plots. The Irrigation Department claims there are 160 households already living there but still plenty of room.

But in reality this resettlement valley does not look so much different from the present one. Oil palm and rubber. Durian and pomelo. Stands of coconut and betel. Plantations of mature coffee bushes. Flower gardens. The only empty spaces are hilltops. How many people are here? Around fourteen hundred households with a house registration. Maybe another two or three thousand without. Numbers are difficult because this is the frontier. The core settlers came from adjacent areas of Chumphon some twenty years ago. Others are northeasterners who arrived in the 1980s, or with the logging companies after Typhoon Gay. The neatly gridded resettlement map is a hopeless dream. What will happen if the government really does move the other villagers here? A fifteen-year resident readying cut flowers for the Bangkok market replies with great elegance and discretion: "I think I will have many new friends. But we will all have to go a little hungry."

The tradeoff is not easy. The floods in Chumphon town are bad and costly. The government offices, built alongside the river, go under water too. But damming this valley is not the only way or even the best way. A royal project to divert the flood water into "monkey cheeks" has just been completed. The province is proud of it. Already the project site is part of tourist itineraries. The municipality is cutting and renovating other canals to improve drainage. These schemes should already take care of flooding in normal years. Last year Chumphon did not flood. With some planned extensions, they might take care of bad years too.

And when a typhoon makes a direct hit, nothing is going to work. The Irrigation Department assesses the dam scheme through the economics of costs and benefits: what is the value of the benefits of flood control and irrigation; what are the costs of construction and resettlement? But this thinking dates from the era when Thailand had plenty of free land. Agricultural tracts destroyed could be reproduced elsewhere. People could be moved with only minor inconvenience. But that is no longer true. The Chumphon provincial forestry officer admits there is really no resettlement land available.

The district officer hangs on to the old thinking. "If this dam is necessary," he argues, "we will just have to find somewhere to move these people. If there is nowhere in Chumphon, then in Ranong, Surat, or Nakhon. If it is necessary, we will simply have to do it." But in these other provinces, the land situation is no different. Because of this lack of land, the tradeoff is no longer a simple cost-benefit exercise. It is human. And political.

The floods in Chumphon town are bad, but they usually last no more than two to three days. Building the dam will change the life of the villagers permanently. The provincial governor seems sensitive to this human calculus. "If we move the villagers," he insists, "their situation must be no worse than before."

Such sensitivity is new. It has not arisen by magic or by chance. It has been created by the strength of the villagers' opposition. "When we started," says one of the leaders, "we thought we had no chance of success." The Irrigation Department promised to ride roughshod over them, as it had done elsewhere. It told them it was planning an *ang kep nam* (reservoir) which sounded small, undisruptive, even useful. The villagers found out by themselves that it was really a dam which would flood the whole valley. "Each time you are fooled," one of the leaders says with a grin, "you become a little cleverer." They joined forces with the Assembly of the Poor which forced the government to place the project under review. They made the provincial officials agree to stay out of the area during the review. Some officials who strayed in were "arrested" and delivered back to the district office. The protesters clubbed together to buy the plot of land where the Irrigation Department wants to site the dam. At meetings with officials, they bring along cameras and cassette-recorders to make a record. The fertility of the valley has provided the villagers with both the incentive and the funds to mount an effective challenge.

The Irrigation Department still plans projects as if land is freely available, as if displaced people can be relocated into neatly gridded resettlements, as if the costs can be factored into the calculation of the project's return. But there is no free land. So the costs are not simply financial but human, social, and ultimately political. The calculation of feasibility goes beyond simple arithmetic.

Standing on a hilltop overlooking this extraordinarily fertile valley, one of the villagers says thoughtfully: "Isn't it strange we have to fight our government to save our land?"

HOW MUCH IS A TREE WORTH?

30 September 1999

How much is a tree worth? For example, one of the golden teak trees in the Mae Yom National Park. Simple, you might say. What would you get if you cut it down and sold the timber?

But lots of trees together in a forest have other values. They create an environment for lots of other plants and animals—including fungi, shoots, herbs, insects, and game which villagers collect, consume, and sell. Cut down the trees, and these other things disappear too.

They also create an environment which is pleasant to visit, and which can have value for tourism. As the coverage of forest dwindles, these sites become rarer and more valuable.

They also help the planet. Forests store carbon. Every hectare chopped down releases more carbon into the atmosphere and adds to global warming.

They are also a stock of biodiversity—especially areas like the Mae Yom Park, "the best natural teak forest in Thailand." The high-value golden teak is a unique result of the local soil and other environmental conditions. Of course, there are other teak forests elsewhere. But cutting down any of them statistically reduces the potential for maintaining or improving the future quality of teak production. In the case of the exceptional Mae Yom golden teak, this reduction is more than usual.

Finally, many people who will never visit Mae Yom may still want it to exist and be available for their kids and their kids' kids to enjoy. Doesn't this desire also have some value?

Cutting down the trees destroys all these other values—the forest produce, the tourism potential, the contribution against global warming, the biodiversity store, the legacy for future generations.

But when the government wants to cut down trees to build a dam, road, or pipeline, it calculates only the cubic meters of timber. If the irrigation or electricity provided by the dam is worth more than the timber lost, then cost-benefit accounting says the dam should be built.

This has bothered environmentalists for some time. It means the authorities go on building dams and other projects which would not get built if these other values entered into the accounting. Villagers lose their income from gathering forest products. The future costs of rectifying global warming increase. The potential for tourism and other future uses is destroyed. The gene pool shrinks.

But the problem is that these other values are difficult to calculate. Estimating the cubic meters of timber is relatively simple. Putting a value on the contribution to global warming is a lot more difficult.

But now an attempt has been made. The work is a team effort between Thai and international academics, headed by Dr. Khunying Suthawan Sathirathai.[29] It focuses on the Kaeng Sua Ten dam project in the Mae Yom National Park in Phrae. It combines the sweat of field research and the sophistication of econometric modeling. And the results are both shocking and hopeful.

To calculate the value of forest products, the team spent a year interviewing villagers. Some two thousand households are involved in gathering forest produce. The main ten products sold in the market in significant quantities—four types of mushroom, three varieties of bamboo shoot, two vegetables, and red ants' eggs—deliver a total net income of 72 million baht a year. This more than doubles these households' total income. It is especially important for the poor.

To calculate the potential value of the site for ecotourism, the team designed a series of tourist packages—rafting, elephant treks, hikes, tree study—and surveyed three hundred Thai and two hundred foreign tourists to find out the potential market value, and in particular the additional value conveyed by the teak forest.

To calculate how much people in general value the forest, the team made a survey of 915 people across twelve provinces. They were asked

---

29. *Khrongkan kan suksa lae phatthana kan pramoen kha thang sethasat khong pa mai* (Research project to improve the estimation of the economic value of forest), Centre for Environmental Economics, Chulalongkorn University, 1999.

how much they would give in a one-off *tham bun* (merit-making) donation to preserve the forest for future generations.

On global warming, the team calculated the cost of replanting trees elsewhere to repair the damage done by cutting down the Mae Yom forest. To examine the impact on biodiversity, the team constructed a sophisticated model with pages of econometric equations and computer simulations.

In the area which will be flooded by the Kaeng Sua Ten dam, there are around half a million golden teak trees. In 1991, the dam project calculated the expected future income from sustainable logging and concluded that this forest had a capital value (NPV, fifty years, 5 percent) of 60 million baht. Just 120 baht per tree. In 1997, the Thailand Development Research Institute (TDRI) reworked the data using more realistic pricing and upped the capital value to 400 million, or 800 baht a tree. But this calculation still took account only of the timber, not all the other things.

This new study reckons that the forest, apart from the timber value, has a capital value of 3.8 to 6.4 billion baht, between 7,600 and 12,800 baht per tree.

The largest element (2.2 billion) is the value which people place on keeping this forest in existence for future generations. Next comes the capital value of the forest produce at 1.4 billion (the mid-point estimate). The genetic value is small but still important. The team disagreed on the calculation regarding global warming so the estimates range from very little to almost a billion.

The size of these figures, and the difference from the simple timber estimates used by all other project evaluations, is shocking. It indicates how much damage other projects have done simply because these other costs were not evaluated. The capital value of forest products is especially striking. It is higher than the (generous) estimate of the timber value. Other projects have casually deprived villagers of this resource by simply not attributing it any value.

The figures will, of course, be controversial. This research project is experimental on a world scale. Those in favor of the Kaeng Sua Ten dam have dismissed earlier, less sophisticated challenges as mere "academic exercises." This report will run into the same flak. The people supporting such dam projects have a narrow rather than a broad focus. If the Irrigation Department has no such dam projects, it has no reason to exist, and no under-the-table cashflow. Local politicians want the glory of bringing such projects to fruition. Contractors, timber merchants, and land speculators want profits. None of these people are interested in forest gathering, ecotourism, global warming, or the gene pool.

But this report is also a beacon of hope. Cutting down forests to build dams might have made sense some decades ago when there were lots of forests. But cutting down a forest like Mae Yom now is an act of vandalism on a global scale. This research challenges the cost-benefit accounting which enables such vandalism to continue. The methodology needs to be simplified and applied to other projects which are pending. At the Phong Khun Phet dam project in Chaiyaphum, for example, forest gathering is far more extensive than in Mae Yom. People come from all over the northeast. Putting a value on this gathering would totally change the cost-benefit result.

Recently, Chuan Leekpai indicated that he wanted the Kaeng Sua Ten project to go ahead. If it meant cutting down a forest, he said, then they would just have to plant another one somewhere else.

But forests are more than the sum of their trees. After this report, it is not that simple.

PUBLIC FORUM: A FAILURE, BUT A VICTORY

21 August 2000

How to protect the environment and protect the little people in an era which worships the "creative destruction" of the free market? This is a global problem. Despite the explosion of scientific knowledge, we are smashing up the planet. Despite unprecedented prosperity, the ranks of the world's poor continue to increase.

The Pak Mun dam has become an international issue because it captures this big global problem in a tiny local nutshell. The project was a bad idea, carelessly managed. It has damaged one of the country's major river systems for very little benefit. It hurt a lot of little people who have refused to be ignored. As a result, Pak Mun has become a rallying point for people who want to stop this sort of destruction. Last week, this put five ministers, two hundred aggrieved villagers, twenty television crews, and a thousand observers into a Thammasat University auditorium for a "public forum" on the issues of dams, land, and forests.

The event had great billing. Government spokesmen announced that it would "solve everything." Minister Wattana Asawaheme called it a "historic day." The moderator said this was "a new way to solve problems in Thai society." It seemed many people attended just to be there and to be seen there—the prime minister's secretary, a TV chat show host, the university rector.

But in one sense, the forum achieved nothing. There was no attempt to negotiate a solution on any one of the specific issues up for debate. Both the government representatives and the Assembly of the Poor advisers reeled off their speeches like actors in a well-rehearsed play. After all, who really believed that problems accumulated over decades would be solved in four hours under the spotlight of live TV?

It was a drama with heavy influences from the theater of the absurd. As the participants arrived, they were treated to a video of Mr. Bean. The villagers, identified by pink paper tags, were ushered into the auditorium in a crocodile, like school kids on an outing. The speeches were heard over a soundtrack provided by the constant tinkle-and-beep of personal electronic equipment. The moderator was armed with a sports clock, borrowed from the Asian Games, which timed out speakers with a peremptory buzz. When Savit Bhotivihok failed to make his point within the three-minute limit, he giggled like a game show participant who had just lost the money.

More importantly, the play on view seemed to be a tragedy in which the two sides end up more alienated than ever. Most of the government side read their lines from a script. Several phrases came up time and time again. The national interest. The benefit of everybody. All 60 million people. The country's future. The scriptwriter wanted to emphasize that the Assembly of the Poor and the protesting villagers are a small group of selfish people who are standing in the way of the government's noble efforts to bring prosperity to everybody. We cannot solve land problems of the hill people in the north, said Newin Chidchob, because "90 percent of them are not Thai." This was not a play about harmony and reconciliation, but about self-justification.

More tragic was the growing realization that many on the government side have learned nothing from the Pak Mun affair. Savit Bhotivihok argued that government had spent the money on the dam, so now we just have to use it. In short, it doesn't matter that the benefit is small, the ecological costs are high, and the dam is internationally condemned. Who cares about the Mun River. Deputy agriculture minister, Anurak Jureemat, was panting to build Phong Khun Phet and other irrigation dams whose plans are based on the same bad thinking, bad cost-benefit analysis, and devious evasion of environmental controls as Pak Mun was. This is not the last time we will see this tragedy staged.

To understand why, you had to look at the details of the cast list, costuming, and staging. While the villagers were identified by their pink paper tags, the government people were all identified by those telling little lapel pins. Not all of them were so little. Forestry chief Plodprasob Suraswadi had the biggest and shiniest lapel pin that Chang Noi has ever seen. Wattana Asawaheme came with two impressive models of the senior bureaucrat. Their only role was to sit on either side while he spoke, because every temple-goer knows that a god looks much more powerful with a pair of flanking *thevada*. This was the Assembly of the Gods. Scan down the cast list and read the attending ministers' surnames: Asawaheme, Bhotivihok, Techaphaibun, Chidchob. This was the Assembly of the Rich too. When the framework of an old dictatorial bureaucratic state is taken over by business politicians, then development is very destructive.

But this play is part of a larger drama that has some brighter scenes. Two important things have come out of the Pak Mun mess and the government's recent confrontations with the Assembly of the Poor. The Electricity Generating Authority has committed that Pak Mun is the last hydro dam. It has junked plans to trash other Isan rivers just like the Mun. The Forestry Department has said it will no longer move people out of the forests by force. Plodprasob laid this out in detail. It's no use, he said, evicting 1.2 million people when realistically there is nowhere else to dump them. Some method has to be found to let them stay, but prevent further destruction.

Of course, there are still problems with these commitments. The Irrigation Department still wants to build bad dam projects. The forest land policy sounds fine as policy, but the implementation may be another matter. The government is still trying to evade the local participation and environmental concern mandated by the constitution.

A third victory was the Thammasat forum itself. The only way to oppose destructive development is public pressure. The little people are not admitted to the Assembly of the Gods. Over the last decade, they have created a parliament of the street. With this forum broadcast on live TV, this was for a short time elevated into a parliament of the airwaves.

In the larger scope of things, these are three big victories. The tragic side is that the agitation to achieve these victories has taken about ten years. Almost every day Chuan says to the villagers sleeping on the roads around Government House, go home and we will solve your problems. But the lesson of history is that if you go home, nothing happens. The Assembly of the Gods has its own concerns. As Mot Wanida

Tantiwittayapitak spoke to huge applause, they can rescue a financial system at any cost, but they resist spending peanuts on the problems of the poor. The only way to prevent the government trampling on the little people and trashing the environment is by constant pressure. Many of the protesters have still not got what they want. Their particular problems are too small, too old, or too tricky for the Gods to tackle. But these protesters have contributed to some big victories which will have value for the future.

This is heroism of a kind. Maybe we should think of those pink paper tags as medals.

BUILD THE DAM OR WE'LL DESTROY THE FOREST

5 February 2001

The Thai state is slowly learning how to listen to its citizens. For two days, supporters and opponents of the Phong Khun Phet (PKP) dam in Chaiyaphum aired their views before an independent panel. It was not a "public hearing" because these have become exercises in conflict. Rather it was just "collecting opinions." Five to seven hundred people came to listen. Seven local groups aired their views. The only moment tinged with violence came when the district officer jabbed his finger angrily at the chairman over a point of procedure.

PKP is not a big project. In fact it's tiddly—a small earth dam with a modest target of increasing irrigation down the upper Chi River. But it has become a big issue. A handful of villages which live from gathering forest products will be flooded out. They opposed the project. Environmentalists supported them. The forest is not lush, but it's one of the last sites of the *bai lan*, the tree whose fiber was once used as paper. Over three years ago, the project was put on hold.

The supporters spoke first. Villagers who live just downstream from the dam site have real reasons to support it. This area lies in rain shadow. Even in the monsoon, they can lose the whole crop because the rain disappears for two weeks. In the dry season, cropping is impossible. Villagers go off to factories and construction sites. PKP promises to turn them from precarious single-croppers into comfortable double-croppers. They want it badly.

A second group also supports. Over the last five years, Chaiyaphum town has flooded badly. This rarely happened before. Last year it happened three times, and the floodwaters stayed a long time. Townspeople suffered and lost money. They believe the PKP dam will hold back the floodwater.

This urban support changes the politics. The townspeople are more sophisticated, more monied, more influential. They have new arguments in favor of the dam. It will attract tourists who will generate income.

The third group of supporters is more sinister—the local politicians and men of influence. The hearing is supposed to be a platform for those directly affected, but somehow these people climb onto the agenda. They add nothing new, but repeat the arguments. More first crop. More second crop. No flooding. More tourist income. Their grasp of local reality is so poor that a villager has to cut in and correct one speaker's basic geography. But their participation sends a message. There are interests at stake other than irrigation, floods, and *bai lan*. Important things like land speculation and construction contracts. The local MP turns up in his shiny 4-wheel-drive and his flashy brand-name shirt. He is an enthusiastic supporter. He has just leapt nimbly from New Aspiration to Thai Rak Thai. He doesn't come in to listen but lingers outside. He is a presence. Some of the supporters come out for a quiet conversation.

Then comes the threat. The last speaker among the supporters is worried that the panel might actually listen to the opponents. They will tell you lies, he says. There is no environmental value. The forest is gone already. The *bai lan* are almost finished. The villagers don't really earn an income from forest produce. Besides, if the dam is not built, his co-villagers will go on illegally logging what remains of the forest until there is nothing left for sure.

According to the supporters, all the farmers will become rich, out-migration will cease, the townspeople will keep their feet dry, and the province will be bathed in prosperity. But the extent of irrigation imagined by the various supporters is three to ten times the amount in the plan, and way beyond the capacity of the water stored. The flood prevention was not part of the project design. A few moments of study shows that it's a complete fantasy. At most the dam can hold back 5 percent of the flow in the Chi River. The runoff flooding the town is coming from a different direction. A new bypass is probably damming the runoff and causing the floods. Hopes for tourist income have been generated by TV pictures of trainloads visiting the Pasak dam. The PKP project has become not a dam but a *thevada*, a goddess bringing everything good.

Reality lies just forty kilometers away at Lamkhanchu, a small earth dam like PKP. It was finished four years ago. The benefits claimed were just the same—more first crop, more second crop, more tourist income generation. Downstream there is no sign of flourishing two-crop agriculture, just parched fields of cassava and sugarcane. As with PKP, there was no plan for distributing the water. Throughout this tract, the rivers are cut deep into land, and the geography is not easy for contour channels. Without big pumps and investment in channels, the water won't reach any farms except those on the riverbank. At present the only beneficiary of Lamkhanchu's water is a big cassava factory.

Tourism? There are four pickup trucks parked by the reservoir edge and a few kids splashing about in rubber tires. Even this meager attendance (on a public holiday) is generating no income.

A few meters away are the project's victims. The villagers from the flood zone accepted the offer of money compensation. But the payment was so slow it barely covered the debts they incurred while waiting. Nothing came of the promises of resettlement land. Three to four hundred families are squatting in makeshift bamboo shelters along the road. Another of the refugee camps left behind by development.

PKP was planned in an era when forest still seemed expendable, and people could still find new land. Now both these conditions have vanished. But like the pipelines, power stations, and other dams, the project had gone a long way before civil society became strong enough to demand a proper economic, social, and environmental accounting. By then, more was at stake than irrigation and *bai lan*. Again Lankhamchu gives a hint. The road along the dam crest is riven with splits, hastily repaired. The water level is much lower than expected at this time of year. Is the dam not being properly used because it's substandard? Will the same thing happen at PKP? Why, asked the opponents, has the PKP construction contract been awarded to a company with a phantom address in a pharmacy shop in Ratchaburi?

BLAST THE MEKONG

23 September 2002

In December this year, government was planning to start blasting the bed of the Mekong River in Chiang Rai to create a channel for larger shipping. The project is now on hold. But it has the look of another Pak Mun disaster on a much, much larger scale.

Anyone who has traveled down this stretch of the Mekong from Chiang Saen towards Luang Prabang will know it is crammed with rocks, rapids, shoals, cataracts, and whirlpools. Blasting enough of this away to make room for 300-ton ships will radically change the river. Driving such big ships down the channel will change it again. The stream will flow faster. Water levels will change. Riverbanks will be affected by the flow rate and ships' wake. Fish breeding grounds will be disrupted. All this, in turn, will impact the people who live along both sides.

But the government is telling us the impact will be insignificant. In fact, the government was hoping we wouldn't find out about this at all.

The original plan comes from China which wants to redesign the Mekong River for navigation. In April 2000, government signed an agreement with China (and Burma and Laos). The agreement says any changes must respect local laws. But that's just part of the boilerplate. There was no public discussion, no public hearing, no debate.

No impact assessment was required, but the project went ahead with one for form's sake. The study of this ambitious redesign of a major world waterway took just six months to complete. It concluded that the impact would be insignificant. It blithely states that the project "is acceptable to environment protection laws" in all four countries. The Mekong River Commission condemned this report as "substantially inadequate," "fundamentally flawed," and "not up to international standard." Most of its findings were simply "speculation."

Yet in January of this year, cabinet approved the plan to dynamite rapids—eleven in the first stage, and another fifty-one later. Some preliminary blasting was carried out. Then the word started to get out.

Projects like Pak Mun, Bo Nok, and Hin Krut started in the dark ages. When they were challenged, government shuffled its feet, looked at the ground, acted embarrassed and said, sorry, this was all fixed under the old rules; let's just have a nice public hearing and get on with it.

But the Mekong blasting originated in the era of the 1997 Constitution and the Freedom of Information Act. Local communities are supposed to have a say about what happens on their doorstep. Information is supposed to be available. The environment is supposed to be valued enough that nothing big is done without proper study. But the Mekong blasting started with no local consultation, no public announcement, no public hearing, no proper study.

Once the news was out, civil society swung into action. NGOs dug information out of the deep mines where government had buried it. Activists published preliminary studies about the impact on the riverbanks, fish breeding, plant life, and fishing communities. Local people put together a petition. A Senate subcommittee visited Chiang Rai in June and called for the project to be halted.

The response again came right out of the dark ages. The minister responsible (transport and communications) kept his mouth shut. The prime minister looked the other way. The Asian Development Bank (ADB), which has made Mekong development one of its specialties, gazed on stoically. A heroic example of the ostrich defense gambit.

Then the activists found a chink in the armor. Suppose the blasting altered the river course. That might change the national boundary which has never been properly mapped and hence runs down the middle of the main channel. There was a stunning risk that a few rocks might change from "Thailand" into "Laos." This information was sent to the defense minister. Reacting valiantly to this threat to the national boundary, General Chavalit had the project suspended.

Attacks on local communities and on the environment could be ignored. An attack on "the nation" (or at least, a few of its wet rocks), could not. But realism suggests this suspension is only temporary and cosmetic. China is behind the project. Chavalit is friends with China. Some work-around will be found before too long.

What does this incident tell us about life in the new post–dark age of the People's Constitution and the Freedom of Information Act?

Government can still sign international agreements, pass cabinet resolutions, authorize inadequate impact studies on a big project with big potential impact, without consulting people who will be affected.

The Senate reacted to the issue. But where were the local MPs, the representatives of the people? It's probably significant that the Chiang Rai Chamber of Commerce is very keen on the Mekong navigation project. Its member like the prospect of more river trade and tourism. One of the fishermen roused against the project said: "I really think these business people are the 'never have enough' people. They might have a 100 million baht now, but they still want another 1,000 million baht."

Although the project and the process clearly contravened several sections of the constitution (especially section 56, but also 46, 76, and 79), there is no mechanism to activate the constitution in such a situation.

On a technicality, government was able to evade the 1992 Environment Protection Act, carry out a "patently inadequate" impact assessment, and conduct no public hearing. It is time the 1992 Act was amended. Its scope must be widened so it is not so easy to evade. The process for appointing consultants to carry out impact assessments must be taken away from the offices promoting the project and given to an independent body. These assessments must look at the social as well as environmental impacts. Proper public hearings must be part of the process. Some means must be found to make the courts uphold the constitution.

There are few strategies of environmental defense dodgier than relying on General Chavalit.

WATER MANAGEMENT IN A HAZE

19 March 2007

The forests are smoldering. The north is choking on the haze. In the background, you can hear a rustling sound. Bureaucrats are dusting off big-budget proposals for rescuing Thailand from drought. As background, it's worth looking at the recent history.

Four years ago, the National Water Resource Committee announced a grand vision that would relieve poverty, make deserts bloom, and "turn Thailand into an agricultural powerhouse." Behind the vision was a simple idea. Water would be taken away from places where there was too much, and given to places where there was too little. The results expected were little less than astounding. Over the past two hundred years, the engineers had brought irrigation to only 22 million out of 131 million rai of farmland. But under this new project, the irrigated area would be doubled in five years, and quadrupled eighteen years after that. Virtually every farmer was promised tap water and enough for farming.

The scale, the vision, and the promise were eye-catching. The Thaksin government further raised the project's profile by branding it as the Water Grid, brilliantly borrowing the metaphor of the electricity distribution system. It was easy to imagine water flowing all around the country as power now flows from the rows of great striding pylons down to the tangled cabling on every street.

Everything about the project was big. The minister announced that 30 or 40 million people would benefit. The number of new reservoirs to be dug would exceed twenty-five thousand. The amount of earth-moving required was enough to excite every construction contractor and truck owner in the land. The length of piping was incalculable. And the total cost figure had both scale and elegance: a cool 5 billion US dollars.

Such scale generates its own momentum. The environment minister who mumbled doubts about the whole thing was soon packing his bags. His successor bypassed the usual procedures for public hearings and other forms of scrutiny. Academics who raised objections were brushed aside. When Pramote Maiklad, a former irrigation chief and key figure in royal irrigation projects, suggested the scheme was "not cost-effective nor feasible in terms of engineering techniques," he could not be heard above the chorus of salivation.

The main obstacle to the project was not the critics but the enthusiasts. In the rush to get a piece of the action, different groups jammed up the doorways. The Irrigation Department and the Department of Water Resources came up with rival versions of the scheme. The two agencies had to convene a peace conference as their infighting threatened to derail the whole sumptuous scheme.

While the project was big on vision, big on political value, big on budget, big on benefits for the agencies involved, and big on profits for contractors, it lacked a few important elements. Most of all, it simply lacked enough water.

The biggest benefit was expected in the poor dry northeast. The amount of rain which falls in the region and fills the local rivers is simply not enough to spread around. Way back in 1956, consultants concluded that the only way to irrigate Isan would be to use water from the Mekong. But the dam proposed at that time would have displaced almost half a million people, and the scheme had to be dropped. All subsequent irrigation projects in the northeast have attempted to use the little water available locally with a bit more efficiency. But they have not been very successful. The Rasi Salai dam increased salination of the soil and prompted big local protests. The Pak Mun scheme wrecked local fisheries and provoked national protests. Similar schemes on the Songkram River were howled down. Weir projects along the Chi River are underutilized because farmers don't think it worth paying for the water. Similar projects along the Mun were abandoned because the estimated rate of return was too low. Many of the ponds built under the Green Isan project are useless.

Where to find the water? The Water Grid quietly hoped to suck the water out of Laos. It planned to build dams on rivers inside Laos, and pump the water through a pipe *under* the Mekong. Similarly in the north, the Water Grid planned to get water from the Salween River in Burma. Even among the boosters of the scheme inside the bureaucracy there were many people who doubted such diversion schemes would ever be politically acceptable.

But water was not the only thing lacking. Irrigation only brings a benefit if there are people to use the water. But people are draining away from Isan. Because there is too little labor, farmers have shifted to using labor-saving methods like broadcasting, hired mechanical harvesters, and brought in workers from Laos. More water is unlikely to reverse the trend of out-migration. In addition, the areas expected to be irrigated by the Grid in Isan are vulnerable to salination. For these and other reasons, the projected returns on public investment in irrigation in Isan are hopelessly low. It makes far more sense to invest in education, electricity, roads, or agricultural research.

The Water Grid was a very big idea that made very little sense. Parts of the project were excellent, but the whole thing got overblown. The point here is not to condemn the Thaksin government. The problem existed long before, and will continue after. With the fall of Thaksin, the Water Grid may be dead, but its ghost is already walking. On the first signs of this year's drought, the Irrigation Department promptly claimed "more dams are needed," and vaunted its scaled-down version of the Grid scheme.

Water management is hugely important for Thailand. With global warming and local environmental decline, the oscillation between drought and flood is getting worse. But the potential profits from water management schemes tend to distort the process of research and planning. Bureaucrats, politicians, consultants, and contractors have mutual interests in blocking proper public scrutiny. Scale takes over sense. And the haze gets worse.[30]

---

30. This article summarized research by François Molle and Philippe Floch, appearing as "Megaprojects and social and environmental changes: The case of the Thai 'Water Grid,'" *Ambio*, 37, 2, April 2008.

Culture and custom

CULTURAL REVOLUTION IN THAILAND

29 August 1996

At a recent seminar, a leading Thai intellectual compared "Thai culture" to a detergent. Both are packaged up for easy consumption. But with detergents there is a choice of brands. And the consumer has a chance to say what he or she thinks about the product, as seen in many detergent adverts.

There is a cultural revolution under way. It has been brewing for at least a decade, but now is reaching a critical phase. The roots of this revolution lie in the experience of the Chinese immigrants to Thailand.

Most urban families have some Chinese origins. There are no exact figures, but very few could claim to have no immigrant ancestor. Most are second- or third-generation descendents of the million plus migrants who arrived between the 1920s and the 1940s.

The rulers welcomed these migrants as long as they abandoned their Chinese culture and "became Thai." That meant giving up Chinese names, Chinese schooling, and the use of Chinese language in public.

It also meant accepting a particular package of Thai culture, with three main parts. First, Thais are the main branch of a big racial family scattered across Southeast Asia. Second, Thai history revolves around the successive kingdoms of Sukhothai, Ayutthaya, and Bangkok. Third, Thai culture is a mix of the royal and the rural—the arts and rituals of the court, and the crafts and beliefs of the peasant.

This package left no room for other race origins, other histories, and for the whole urban cultural tradition. It is this package which the cultural revolution is out to overthrow.

For many decades, most Chinese immigrants were happy to buy this package as the price of their admission to Thailand. After all, other countries in the region demanded higher prices and tougher terms. Many Thai-Chinese were so pleased with the deal that they became enthusiastic supporters of Thai culture. A lot took personal pride in the story of Thai origins and history, even though their own origins were elsewhere. Some even went on to crusade for the "Thai" nation against the threat posed by the "Chinese." Luang Wichit Wathakan wrote up the Thai race mythology and campaigned for a "Thai economy for the Thai people." Phya Anuman Rajadhon documented Thai cultural practice. Sulak Sivaraksa defended Thai traditions against the modern world. Chai-anan Samudavanija analyzed the special character of Thai political traditions. All had Chinese origins.

For many decades, Thailand's rulers suppressed anything Chinese. Mainly they were worried about the import of Chinese politics, particularly during the communist era. As the Cold War softened and dissolved, so did this fear. In the 1970s, some leading figures started to rediscover their Chinese origins. The great academic and administrator, Puey Ungphakorn, said he was proud of his Chinese ancestry. The politician and artist, Kukrit Pramoj, recognized that he had a Chinese grandmother. But at this stage, there was nothing aggressive about these claims. Puey emphasized that he was first and foremost a Thai. Kukrit remained unmistakably a traditional Thai aristocrat.

In 1986, Nidhi Eoseewong wrote a history of Taksin, the king of Thonburi whose fourteen-year reign immediately preceded the 1782 foundation of Bangkok. Taksin had been virtually written out of the standard histories, and was said to have gone mad. Nidhi made clear that Taksin was Chinese by origin, claimed that Taksin was a great man, and portrayed him as a liberal and enlightened ruler whose "madness" was probably a historical invention by those who overthrew him.

Nidhi's Taksin was an attack on the official version of Thai culture. Moreover, Nidhi presented the whole book as a manifesto for granting more recognition to the role of the Chinese in Thai history. He argued that there was a specific culture of the Chinese-in-Thailand. To distinguish Chinese-in-Thailand from Chinese-in-China he used the word "*jek*." Until then, "*jek*" had been a slang and sneering term for Chinese immigrants (rather like "chink").

Around the same time, Sujit Wongthet described Thai culture as "*jek bon lao*," Chinese mixed with Laotian. He claimed he couldn't make head or tail of the official version of Thai society, history, and culture. As far as he could see, the two biggest elements in the demography and the culture were Chinese immigrants and Laotian peasants.

The use of the word *jek* by Nidhi and Sujit was shocking and challenging. The official version of Thai culture simply blotted out the Chinese immigrants, their large numbers, their extraordinary history, their big contribution to modern Thailand. Nidhi implied that any version of Thainess which ignored the *jek* was incomplete, wrong, and offensive to a lot of people.

Over the last ten years, this "*jek* tendency" has spread. Now it includes not only revisionist historians like Nidhi, but students of urban culture, economists who concentrate on the city and ignore the countryside, and political scientists who analyze Bangkok society. At a recent government-sponsored conference on new directions among Thai intellectuals, the "*jek* tendency" was clearly dominant, and the attack on "Thainess" very strong. Kasian Tejapira said he felt "raped" by Thainess. Nidhi compared Thainess to "a product that doesn't sell."

At another conference run by the Fine Arts Department, the historian Charnvit Kasetsiri noted that history in the universities had become turgid and boring, but outside academia, history was controversial and fascinating. Drawing a deep breath, he added that "*jek* history" was especially exciting and important.

This is all heady intellectual stuff. But the same trends are running through popular culture, too. The biggest hit TV drama series of the early 1990s was *Lod Lai Mangkon* (the pattern of the dragon). The plot traced one immigrant entrepreneur from Chinatown street smart in the 1940s to successful tycoon and dynast in the 1980s. The story was a thinly veiled mix of the real history of some of Bangkok's well-known families. Millions of viewers found echoes in their own personal histories. Dramatized on prime-time TV, watched by millions, discussed by critics, and talked about by everyone, the series established the *jek* in the popular version of Thailand's modern history and culture.

Just a few weeks ago, in another TV series, *Mongkut Dok Som* (the bridal crown), the first-generation immigrant characters talked to one another in Chinese, with the Thai translation run as subtitles. A few years ago, such realism would have been unthinkable. Now it makes it a bit easier for the Thai-Chinese to take pride in their history.

It is not difficult to see what is driving this trend. The urban economy, driven by the Thai-Chinese, is rampant. Mainland China is no longer a political threat but a great economic opportunity.

Around the world, globalization has provoked a resurgence of local identities. In Thailand, this reaction is taking special form, molded by Thailand's special history. Some descendents of the immigrant Chinese are complaining that the official version of Thai history and culture has simply blotted them out. But they are not trying to dig out a "Chinese" identity. Rather they want to rehabilitate the history of the Chinese-in-Thailand. They are very happy they came to Thailand. They want some recognition for the contribution they have made. They want to redefine "Thai culture" as something more like the melting pot which it really is. "A society which is powerful," wrote Nidhi, "allows variety in ways of life and values. The *jek* add to the cultural richness of Thai society."

BANGKOK INVADED BY SONGS AND LAUGHTER

12 April 1997

Big changes in society often first come to light in entertainment and popular culture. The writers, performers, and media entrepreneurs are sensitive to the seismic trends below the social surface.

Over the past two decades, Bangkok's popular culture has been molded by the growing size and prosperity of the new middle class. Everything has been modern, urban, glossy, slick. The most important media have been television dramas, lifestyle magazines, and the light pop music pioneered by Grammy. All three have reflected the excitements and traumas of creating a new kind of life in a new kind of city.

The lifestyle mags have provided a guide on what to wear, how to behave, who to admire, what to be. The grandmummy of them all, *Dichan*, translates appropriately as "I." The TV drama serials have ranged across the spectrum of the new city life. Students learning about life in a new world. Families wrestling with the complications of growing prosperity. Women balancing careers and families. New entrepreneurs braving the shark-infested waters of Bangkok business. The songs of Grammypop have been about romance, but also about growing up in a new world, and about urban problems from pollution to prostitution.

Through all three—TV dramas, lifestyle magazines, and pop music— the dominant figure has been the new star, performing as actor, singer, and model. Usually a Thai-farang *luk khrueng*. Young, bright, optimistic, well-mannered. These stars are not distant icons, but idealized versions of the boys and girls next door, close enough to be role models for all the absolute beginners of the new city.

This trend is still dominant, though it is becoming a little mechanized, jaded, repetitive. There are just too many *Dichan*-copycat magazines, predictable TV dramas, cookie-cutter Grammypop stars. The time is right for an invasion.

For decades, people have been migrating from the villages to Bangkok and the big provincial towns. In the last few years, they have been coming in larger numbers, staying more permanently, settling in. They bring along their local music. Once in the city, the lives of the migrants change. New jobs. New wealth. New problems. The music changes too. New technology. New influences. New concerns to reflect.

Phleng luk thung (country music) grew out of this process in the 1960s, when migrants from the central region first came to Bangkok in large numbers. The style was created by mixing central-region folk music with the new electric keyboards and with some Latino rhythms and stagecraft popular in the international films and TV shows of the era. The songs were often specifically about the life experience of the migrant, missing the village life back home, struggling with the strangeness and unfriendliness of the city, grasping at new opportunities. With the new technology of cassette tapes, radio, and roadshows touring the country's new highway network, *phleng luk thung* developed a national audience.

Phleng phuea chiwit (music for life) developed in the 1970s by a similar route among a different social group. For the first time, students from the provinces were sucked into Bangkok's colleges and universities in large numbers. Some student musicians from the northeast mixed their local riffs and rhythms with borrowings from country'n'western and rock music. The songs were shaped by the social conscience and political awakening of the decade. The resulting *phleng phuea chiwit* became the soundtrack for political protest.

Despite their vitality and popularity, neither of these styles penetrated the urban mainstream. *Phleng luk thung* was too rural, *phleng phuea chiwit* too political. In the 1980s, they were pushed aside by the surge of slick, modern, international, optimistic Grammypop. By 1990, many of the big *luk thung* troupes had stopped touring. Most of the famous singers had retired. Both the big *phuea chiwit* bands, Caravan and Carabao, had stopped recording, squabbled among themselves, and disbanded.

But in the 1990s, this decline was suddenly and spectacularly reversed. The music found a new audience. And moved towards the urban mainstream.

In 1992, the premature death and emotional funeral of Phumphuang Duangjan revealed the extraordinary range of popularity for this "queen" of *phleng luk thung*. The enthusiast and archivist, Jenphop Jop-krabuanwan, organized some big concerts which showcased the history and highlights of the genre. These essays in nostalgia were soon over-taken by a true revival. Many new young singers appeared. Some mixed *phleng luk thung* with bits of rock, pop, and rap. Some threw in humor. But others offered a self-consciously traditional and pure version of the sound and style. FM radio stations started to feature *phleng luk thung* shows. Then television, too. Several new music-publishing companies put out classic reissues and new albums. Cassette sales mounted. Per-formers began to make music videos for the new TV shows. The "café" nightspots featuring singers mainly for the migrant audience increased in number and popularity. Grammy took Got, a pretty-boy urban pop star whose career just would not spark, and remodeled him as a new-age *luk thung* artist, with huge success.

In 1994, Channel 7 created a TV drama series adapted from a 1960s film called *Monrak Luk Thung*. The director played the rustic setting as farce and the village characters as country bumpkins, which did not go down so well. But the music was wonderful, and drew in a big TV audience. Two soundtrack tapes sold in millions. The urban actors who played and sang the main roles were converted into country singers, earning more from appearing in touring provincial roadshows than from doing yet another TV family drama.

In 1996, a *luk thung* singer who shunned publicity because he felt he looked too downright rural produced a huge national hit. Monsit Khamsoi's *Sang nang* (while I'm away) was played everywhere from country concerts to trendy Bangkok music halls. All other singers had to learn it because it always came up in the request section. Businessmen crooned it at parties and karaoke. The Bangkok Symphony Orchestra made a cover version. Monsit appeared at discos, on TV talk shows, and in glossy magazines. *Phleng luk thung* had arrived in the heart of urban culture.

Phleng phuea chiwit went through a similar resurgence. First the old albums started to sell well again. Then the old singers received more and more requests to appear at clubs, pubs, concerts, and festivals. Ad Carabao made a solo album which outsold many of the Grammy stars, and gained fans beyond Thailand on the new Asian satellite music stations. The Carabao group reformed, recorded new songs, started to tour. Caravan followed suit.

Then the music made a step up to a new urban subculture. First some rustic bars were rechristened as *phuea chiwit* pubs. Then several huge new nightspots, each accommodating several thousand people, appeared under the same label. Many new bands appeared to perform in these venues. *Phleng phuea chiwit* now reached a much wider audience than it had in the 1970s. Still, the students. Also many of the new upcountry migrants. Plus some who deserted the discos and the yuppie Royal City Avenue bars for the *phuea chiwit* pubs, moving out of a glossy world of neon and chrome into a deliberately understated environment of wood and simplicity.

Comedy was not far behind. Along with music, comedy had always been one way the village migrants dealt with the city—laughing at themselves and their new surroundings. The first Bangkok cafés featuring northeastern comics had appeared in the 1960s. But from the late 1980s, the numbers and audiences expanded rapidly. Several venues became rich and famous. People who had come to the city and done well liked to show off their wealth by entertaining friends in these places and patronizing the performers. Many could now make a living touring around these venues as solo comics and members of comic troupes.

Then this upsurge in comedy made the leap into TV. Before the early 1990s, it was hard to find much laughter in the box. A few review style programs had some short-term success. And a handful of comics had support roles in game shows and talk shows. Then some channels tentatively experimented with bringing the café-style format onto the small screen. The audience went for it. All the stations quickly competed to offer comic shows. The popular troupes were hired for corporate and society events. A few figures became household names. The extraordinary Note became a one-man comic industry, selling books, tapes, and concert seats by the millions.

The TV drama, lifestyle magazine, and manufactured pop are still around and still doing well. But they have been shifted slightly to one side by a wave of songs and laughter rolling in from the provinces. Beneath these waves there are seismic shifts in the society, as new groups find their own voice and place in Thailand's modern society.

NATIONALISM IN THE NOODLE SHOP

24 October 1997

Last week Chang Noi was in a noodle shop near the stock exchange. These financial types are only just getting used to these cramped places with no air-conditioning, so they seemed rather overheated and talked loud enough to be overheard ...

Bill: What a mess. What a fudge. The financial rescue package was completely watered down. The finance companies have been given another chance when most of them should be closed down. All the tough rules and regulations have been delayed for two to three years. The foreigners can buy up to 100 percent, but only for ten years. The government is still protecting the local finance bosses who caused all the mess. The country will pay.

Chai: True. It is a mess. But you know a lot of us felt the foreign banks were hoping the package would be really tough because they would benefit. It would provoke a fire sale, and the foreigners would be able to buy up everything cheap. We thought you were goading the government to make the package tough for your own benefit.

Bill: But you're bankrupt. What's the alternative? Rescuing all those lovable financial tycoons with money stolen from the people's pockets? Some solution. Isn't it better to let the foreigners buy in? The people don't have to pay, and you get a better financial system.

Chai: We're not sure about the last part. We liberalized a little bit, and we got this mess. If we liberalize more, maybe we get an even bigger mess.

Bill: But you liberalized so badly. Pegged exchange rate. No controls. Lots of political interference. The result was all this profligate lending to property speculators and over-ambitious dreamers.

Chai: But why do we get all the blame? It takes two to tango. You foreigners lent us all this cheap money. It's very difficult to say no to someone lending you cheap money. Now you blame us for using it badly. But we were new at this game. You were not. The big international finance houses have done this same thing in many countries. How come they lent so much for so long? What were you all thinking about back in 1993 when the average price-earnings ratio on the stock exchange was pushing thirty? You thought it would go up further? Right up to the middle of last year, the money was tumbling in. How come no big international finance house said: this doesn't look like such a good idea.

Bill: You're exaggerating.

Chai: No I'm not. Look back at 1995. Every week someone from an international finance or broking firm was announcing that the fundamentals of the Thai economy were still good, the long-term prospects were still sound, the market downtrend was reversible. You guys have very short memories. Now it's all our fault.

Bill: So you're blaming us for your mistakes?

Chai: No. Of course we did it badly. But I resent that the international financial houses refuse to take any share of the blame. Often the foreign lenders were more careless than the local ones. Look at the fights now going on over some of the property companies. The Thai finance companies lent against collateral. The foreigners lent clean. Now the foreigners are complaining that the Thais are ganging up against them, and that foreign lenders are being discriminated against. Actually, they are trying to accuse the Thais of nationalism to cover up their own mistakes.

Bill: Ah, nationalism. So you're on Mahathir's side. You think this is all a conspiracy to reimpose colonial control.

Chai: Not in those words. But a lot more Asians admire what Mahathir has said than you would like to think. He touches a chord. Westerners need to understand that. Scoffing at Mahathir doesn't help.

Bill: But calling Soros a moron doesn't help either. Soros is just market forces in human form. I thought Thais were all in favor of liberalization and globalization. But I suppose that was when globalization was running your way. Now we have people like that TRIS man who is out on the streets welcoming the freedom of the new constitution one day, then up in arms against freeing up the financial market to admit foreigners on the next. You can't have it both ways.

Chai: But remember when the Arabs were buying into the US banks, and the Japanese were buying up Hollywood? The American press was horrified (actually more about Hollywood than about the banks, but then this was the USA). Was this the death knell of Western capitalism? Can't we stop it? What's the difference here?

Bill: Probably none. But this nationalism thing is dangerous.

Chai: I agree. But again there are two sides. I suspect a lot of Westerners have got fed up with being told about Asian miracles. Last year even Governor Patten of Hong Kong came out to say Britain should follow an "Asian model." I can understand that this was getting very tiresome. The language of Asian success was so aggressive too—all about tigers and dragons. I think this has made many Westerners react with glee at this crisis. An Asian slump restores the proper order of things, with Westerners telling Asians where they went wrong and how they could do better in the future. The problem is, these attitudes stir deep feelings. Both sides need to own up to this.

Bill: But getting defensive and nationalist isn't going to help Malaysia, Thailand, or any other stumbling Asian economy. Turning inwards you get . . . well, you get Snoh Thienthong.

Chai: True. And there's bigger reasons why you and I should not get emotional over all of this. Finance is only the froth. Beneath all of these market forces which are tossing us around, there are bigger social and economic forces churning. Why did all this money flood out of the West to Asia? In the West, you had a rich aging population and the collapse of the welfare state. The result: huge pension funds. You also had the business cycle on the downturn, so the fund managers were looking elsewhere. In Asia you had a poor young population ready to work hard. And a business cycle on the upswing. So the money came flooding out. I can remember these London fund managers ringing me up saying: I've got all this money, can't you help me do something with it. Many times. Just a couple of years ago.

Now the cycles are going the other way. The Western financial markets are airborne. Asia's on the downswing. So the money flows back. Behind all the shouting, that's the story.

Bill: So finance is just thrashing around in the froth? I thought we financiers ruled the world.

Chai: You probably do. Maybe the problem is that these money flows mean different things to you and to me. For Western finance, Thailand is a bit of a sideshow. Somewhere to have a flutter with your funny money. So you put the money in and then you take it out. For you, it's not such a big deal. But for us, the same inflow and outflow is a big deal. It knocks our tiddly little financial system all over the place. We do get a little distraught.

Bill: But why should we stay? Look around you and give me one good reason.

Chai: I can't. But it's like you're saying: "We're taking our money away because we don't like it here any more. We'll stay only if you let us buy up your banks." And we're saying to ourselves: "Do we have to deal with these ungracious people. If we go along with this now, it will be the same for evermore."

KING CHULALONGKORN'S CRISIS
AND TODAY'S CRISIS

26 December 1997

Last week the Siam Society held a seminar to commemorate the centenary of King Chulalongkorn's first visit to Europe. Hosted by this august cultural institution and officially opened by Princess Sirindhorn, the seminar promised a glimpse into history.

Instead, the seminar turned out to be much more about today, the present, the economic crisis.

The parallels were simply too strong. In the 1890s, Siam was threatened by the colonial designs of the British and French. Today Thailand is besieged by international banks, multinational companies, world-scale speculators, and vulture funds. In the 1890s, Siam's sovereignty was at stake. Today, the ownership of much of the Thai economy is at stake. As the former deputy prime minister, Virabongsa Ramangkura told the meeting, there is little difference between the nineteenth-century European traders who demanded Siam open up its markets, and the World Trade Organization's current demands for liberalization. Once again, a small country is under threat from big forces outside.

King Chulalongkorn is revered for steering Siam through the crisis of a hundred years ago, evading the clutches of the colonialists, and engineering the internal reforms which enabled Siam to survive. The chairman of the seminar, Vichit Suraphongchai, opened the event by drawing an explicit parallel between the successful leadership provided by Chulalongkorn in the 1890s crisis, and the need today for leaders with the vision and clout to enforce internal change on a similar scale. Globalization, argued Vichit, is big, accelerating, irresistible. Just as Chulalongkorn recognized the power of Europe and modernized Siam for survival, so Thailand today must recognize the powerful forces of globalization and reform internally to cope with them.

"How capable and ready are our leaders," Vichit asked, "to implement the changes necessary to prepare Thailand for the future?"

But as the seminar evolved over two days, the comforting prospect that Siam could again be saved from disaster by enlightened leadership came under challenge.

Is "leadership" the key to overcoming today's crisis? "The problem of great leaders," noted Somsak Xuto, "is that they are difficult to follow. The seed doesn't take root in the cool shade of a large banyan tree."

The historian Thongchai Winichakul took this point further. Looking to "leaders" for instant solutions is a form of escapism. We tend to pin our hopes on leaders, but leaders always have limitations. It's important, Thongchai urged, not to obstruct the bigger, creative forces in society. Too often we say that the mass of the people are not ready, not educated. But they are the real dynamism in society. "If we think it difficult to build people of high quality, why do we think it will be easier to create a good leader?"

Is King Chulalongkorn the right inspiration for confronting today's crisis? This is complex, because the image of Chulalongkorn lives on in the present day. It has become the focus of a form of national cult. As Apinan Poshyananda's photographs showed, the image turns up on racks of posters between Bon Jovi and Madonna; on shrines at shops, restaurants, go-go bars, and brothels; among the ranks of Hindu and Chinese deities called upon to provide good fortune; and partnered with images of monks like Luang Por Koon who also offer comforting promises of good fortune. For the mass of people, in other words, Chulalongkorn is not so much an inspiration for leadership in the age of globalization, as part of superstitious belief in the power of fate and fortune. As Surichai Wan'gaeo commented, the idea that development would reduce the role of superstition now belongs to the past. We know instead that development simply turns superstitious practice into a commercial opportunity.

Where lies the real root of the current crisis? An outside threat or an internal problem? The real parallel between the Chulalongkorn era and our own, argued Thongchai, lies in the elite's tendency to chase after rainbows. In the late nineteenth century, the Siamese elite felt threatened not just by gunboats but by the cultural aggression of western Europe which made them feel inferior. Siamese aristocrats wanted to be *siwilai*, a term adapted from "civilized," expressing a yearning to be accepted as full members of the modern world. But being *siwilai* was not the same as being Westernized. It was being what the Siamese elite though being Westernized might be. In other words, an illusion. By definition, an illusion is unattainable. The quest is bound to be unsuccessful. The inevitable result is failure and disappointment.

Today the idea of globalization plays the same role as *siwilai* a century ago. Thai leaders fear they are falling behind in the world, so in Thongchai's words they "scramble out from their undistinguished status in order to stand out ahead and above the crowd . . . by quick wealth and signs of the New Rich."

Kasian Tejapira added, "we don't really know what globalization is, but we think it up ourselves, we want it so much, and we chase after it until we fall over."

The lawyer, Kittisak Prokati, approached this idea of an internal crisis from another angle. He argued that the Chulalongkorn reforms have handed down a very imperfect legacy for modern Thailand. In particular, the rule of law has never taken root. In Europe, popular movements created law codes designed to control abuse of power and exploitation of resources. But this was one model which the Fifth Reign did not adopt from Europe, partly because it would restrict the power of the monarch. Law in Thailand is still seen as a set of rules—to obey and often to evade. Students are still taught about the concept of law in this way, rather than law as an expression of justice.

The crisis today, Kittisak added, is a crisis of ethics. Over the last few years, everybody has tried to get rich by breaking the laws, by cheating. This has created a crisis of freedom. How can you have free markets without the law or ethics that allow free markets to work properly? This problem is deep-rooted in history, in politics, in business. It explains the persistence of violence in society. We need people with the courage to fight against those who abuse freedom for political advantage. Changes in the law, added Amorn Chantrasomboon, will only come after changes in politics. And here the new constitution has only made a small start.

Finally, is it already too late to hope a leader can rescue Thailand? The final speaker in the seminar—and the starkest image—was Virabongsa Ramangkura.[31] Where other speakers came in casual clothes, Virabongsa dressed in dark suit and tie. Where others spoke in spirited and often dramatic fashion, he presented in a funeral-march monotone which reduced the audience to pin-drop silence. He had come, after all, to deliver a speech over a corpse. He had helped to shepherd through the financial decrees which transferred the debts of the dead financial companies to the Thai people. We now live, he warned, with the consequences. The banking sector has already been opened up to foreign ownership. Restrictions on land, businesses, and occupations are likely to follow. And the fire sale of assets is coming soon. Any prospect that we can escape the gunboats of globalization, as Chulalongkorn fended off the gunboats of the French, is already past.

31. After the financial crisis broke, Virabongsa served as deputy prime minister from 15 August to 6 November 1997, and was directly involved in concluding agreements with the IMF.

SMOOTHING THE FUTURE, STIRRING UP THE PAST

26 July 1999

How to be a radical? How to make things change? The 7th International Conference on Thai Studies, held recently in Amsterdam, focused on the theme of Thailand as a civil society. For the four hundred academics and activists who gathered for the event, this resolved into one main issue. Does the explosion of political debate, NGO activism, and enthusiasm for reform of all kinds signify real change in Thai society? Are there really new opportunities to make a difference (over AIDS, the environment, human rights, gender, minorities, political reform) by joining organizations and working with the system to try to change it? Or is all this activity just a sideshow, a distraction? Have the great victories (like the 1997 Constitution) been more symbolic than real? Is the Thai state at heart still so shaped by its absolutist and dictatorial past that any attempt to work with it can end only in dire disappointment or corrupting compromise?

For the generation that dominated the conference, the twin events of October 1973 and October 1976 are the defining moments of Thailand's modern history. Two of the keynote speeches dealt with these events and their impact on the present. And two of the 1970s leaders offered contrasting images of how to be a radical a quarter-century down the road.

Thirayuth Boonmi was a leader of the student revolt against military dictatorship in October 1973. Now he has become a kind of lay abbot. He immerses himself in the texts and practices of modern Thai society and politics. He emerges from his ivory *kuti* once a year to preach a sermon guiding his followers through the world of political illusions in search of a better future. Through the 1990s, he has been largely optimistic about the decline of the military, the growth of political activism, the reform of the constitution. His sermons say: get involved.

But the resulting progress is so slow. To move ahead, Thirayuth preached to the conference, a society needs to have some shared vision on what a better future might look like. Nationalism and Marxism have been tried and rejected. Now the words "civil society" project a vision of reduced state control and greater individual participation. But, Thirayuth wonders, can Thais really imagine such a future? After their history of absolutism and dictatorship, even the words are not available. All the Thai translations of "citizen" are words invented by the state to enforce duties on the people, not rights. The word for "society" (*sangkhom*) originally meant "high society" and has barely lost this meaning of division. All the new words beginning with *pracha*-invented to convey ideas of civil society, popular rights, and people's power are comprehensible to only a small intellectual minority. There are no good Thai terms for things like decentralization. If Thailand is to have a civil society, Thirayuth suggests, it first needs the vocabulary. And his self-appointed job is to create it. Despite the slow progress, Thirayuth is still involved.

Thongchai Winichakul was prominent in October 1976 when the army violently suppressed student radicalism. Since then, he has become the most feted modern Thai historian in the international arena. But he has been removed from Thai society—first by jail, and then by self-exile. He functions now as a distant spirit who resides most of the time in the remote chilly regions of north America. He can be summoned up from time to time only by the proper spirit mediums (conference organizers). He is a disorderly spirit who concentrates the chaotic energies from bad events in the past. His role is to stir things up, to spread doubt, to challenge any slide to complacency, to remind the optimistic reformers just how difficult their task truly is.

While Thirayuth dwelt on the problems of building a future, Thongchai talked about the difficulties of understanding the past. The roots of Thai democracy have become very murky. Originally, the story began with the revolt against absolutism by the People's Party in 1932. But after this movement collapsed into fascism and military rule, this version was forgotten. In its place, a new story traced the origin of Thai democracy back to King Prajadhipok's benevolence in granting a first constitution to the Thai people. One story stresses revolt from below. The other highlights benevolence from above. Which to believe?

Similarly, Thongchai went on, there is difficulty about understanding the great events of the 1970s. Should October 1973 and October 1976 be remembered as two complementary parts of one single movement—a revolt from below against military dictatorship and domination of all kinds? Or are they different? Is 1973 a good story in which the king sided with the students to bring down the military dictators; while 1976 is a bad story in which student radicals went too far in challenging the whole structure of power? Thongchai's suggestion was clear. Is there a limit on what can be achieved from below? Is this the true limit on "civil society"?

In the conference's most fragile moment, Thongchai brought all this together. For years, activists have pressed for a monument to commemorate those who died in the events of 1973 and 1976. Recently, the project has suddenly become possible. But the monument commemorates only 1973. Thongchai hinted this had come about because Thirayuth, in the course of his earnest efforts to build a civil society, now works closely with the great and the powerful. These connections made it possible to overcome opposition to the monument project. But only by sacrificing the memory of 1976. The meaning of this hint was not purely or even mainly personal. Thongchai was pointing to a much bigger danger. Many of the veterans of 1973 and 1976 are now important figures in the day-to-day political life of Thailand. Thirayuth is a thinker. Many others have become MPs. Some are important in business. Several figure in the professions, in academia, in the media. They are working inside the system. They often retain at least some of their youthful zeal for change. But how much can they achieve against a deeply conservative system which is capable of Kremlin-like rewriting of the histories of 1932 and 1973–6?

This same theme echoed through panel after conference panel—on environment, health, rights, minorities, political reform, rural protest. Some said: reform will only come by working alongside state agencies. Others countered: that route leads always to deadening compromise;

the strategy must be to wrest power away from the state to popular hands. The first group replied: but that is hopeless idealism.

The same theme ran through the conference's most dramatic scene. Mee Ju is an Akha woman who participated in the hill people's protest for citizenship rights in Chiang Mai in June. She addressed the conference in an old Dutch church, with the black and silver of her Akha costume standing out against the setting's gloomy grandeur like white fire. She spoke in fluent and articulate Thai, showing off the strings of identity cards, certificates, and medallions which her people had received over the years. These were the product of working with the system and accepting its authority. But none of these trinkets grant true nationality. Rather they are an official way of avoiding doing so. They are certificates of the state's bad faith.

The June protest was broken up by the police. But it may in the long run lead to some change. Mee Ju herself signifies both compromise and protest. She has been through Thai education to master the language of negotiation. Now she wears her traditional dress as a badge of difference and defiance.

Perhaps change really comes from a mixture of earnest cooperation and chaotic protest. Perhaps Thailand needs both its lay abbots (Thirayuth) earnestly working inside the system to plot routes towards the future, and its disorderly spirits (Thongchai) stirring up memories of the past to warn of the dangers of compromise.

THE GREAT WALL OF BANGKOK

10 April 2000

The paddy farmers are closing in. A few weeks ago, the protests about rice support prices were way out there in Nakhon Sawan and Ang Thong. Then they moved to Ayutthaya. And now to Nonthaburi. Right there among the collapsed housing projects.

Defending the city is getting more difficult. During Unctad-X, the authorities headed off an invasion of sugar trucks at the very last moment by agreeing to a deal on price. Just before that the cassava farmers promised to present the city with a bonfire of cassava roots (very fragrant), and were dissuaded by a similar concession. Further back, the dairy farmers set off from Pak Chong towards Bangkok with a herd of cows (even more fragrant) but turned back after one died. At the end of 1998, when the rubber planters threatened to turn nasty, the government gave them 4 billion baht in price support.

We can now see that the Asian financial crisis has had two contradictory effects on Thailand. First, it has made the urban economy much more open, more international, more integrated with the world. A large chunk of the financial industry—banks, brokerages, insurance—has been transferred to foreign ownership. Foreign investment has flooded in five to seven times faster than ever before, all to buy over local companies. You can laugh over this or cry over this. Opinions are pretty divided. But you cannot deny that it has happened. More than ever before, the urban economy is exposed to the tastes, prejudices, money flows, inputs, assistance, and demands coming from the world outside. It has suddenly become fashionable to talk about the "dollar zone" of the Thai economy.

The second impact of the crisis is that the countryside has got more fed up. It bore a lot of the brunt of the downturn. The highest unemployment and biggest income falls have been in the rural northeast, because the only welfare cushion available to the laid-off migrant worker was the village. The farmers have been squeezed between the rising baht costs of imported inputs, and the fall in world prices for crops. The crisis also took away a lot of the mystique of the city as modern, progressive, and superior.

In the past, the city could rely on the countryside to provide cheap labor, cheap food, sites to generate the power the city needs, and places to dump its rubbish. Now this is not so certain. Of course the migrant labor will come flooding back as soon as there are jobs. But just about every new project for a dam, power plant, or waste disposal site now faces local protests. And the vanguard of the price protests has reached the city suburbs.

Many in Bangkok welcome the greater internationalization of the economy. It will bring in technology, make things more efficient, increase consumer welfare, speed up the march towards modernity. The old project to build a local capitalism through "development policy" is dead. It was doomed since the collapse of the Cold War meant the Western powers no longer found any political use in building such local capitalisms. Thailand, the argument goes, will now prosper by being a good host for multinational companies. That's why the national agenda has switched to the reforms in education, legal systems, and environment which Thailand needs to compete as a host for multinationals. The model for this strategy is Singapore. Already Ratprasong is metamorphosing into Orchard Road. Recently Bangkok Municipality officials went to Singapore to learn how they make the city green and pleasant.

But Singapore has worked this hosting strategy so successfully for several reasons, not just greening the city. First, it set up the most elaborate welfare system in the world to make sure that everyone shared in the benefits, not only those directly involved in the "dollar zone." Second, it managed its "democracy" very carefully. Third, it gave away its rural hinterland—to Malaysia.

The last point was crucial. Chang Noi was in Singapore in the late 1980s when the economy (and especially construction) went through a low arc of the cycle. The government simply threw out the thousands of illegal Thai workers who had provided the cheap labor during the previous upswing. Later, when things improved, it eased open the backdoor again, but this time to let in Indonesians because they had become the cheapest available. A thin strip of water, and nationality laws, are great tools for managing the urban labor market. And much else besides. Singapore has never had paddy farmers with *i-taen* staging protests among the HDB blocks in Woodlands or Ang Mo Kio.

For Bangkok, the options are not so easy. The government is not likely to give away the old "Lao provinces" in Lanna and Isan to Laos or anyone else. But at the moment there doesn't seem to be any strategy for handling this, other than negotiating price support deals on the curbsides of major highways. In the absence of any other strategy there will eventually be only one logical conclusion: build the Great Wall of Bangkok to keep the countryside out.

In his recently announced election program, Thaksin Shinawatra included a three-year moratorium for farmers' debts. The proposal brought a howl of dismay from his opponents, and from much of the Bangkok press. It's impractical, they said. It would cost too much.

There is a reason to worry about such a moratorium. Other countries have found that in the long term nobody wants to lend to farmers. But the real reasons for the howl of dismay are deeper. Thaksin's proposal is actually giving the farmers something they have asked for. It just might win him the election. And, most important of all, it brings a rural issue into the heart of national politics. It might give the farmers the bad idea that they could use their vote for real benefit, rather than selling it cheap. Quick! Build the Wall!

BAD NEIGHBORS, WOMAN WARRIORS, AND PADDLES

9 July 2001

Three times over the past one hundred–plus years, little countries have been worried that big countries will gobble them up. In the late nineteenth century, European powers grabbed colonies. In the 1930s and '40s, a few countries thought they had the racial "destiny" to control everyone else. Now, the world's richest nations say weaker economies must submit.

Each time there has been resistance. And each time in Thailand, these movements have had certain themes.

First, though the threat comes from the great powers, Thailand treats its neighbors as the enemies. During the colonial scare, Siam's rulers built up Burma as the threat which required Siam to be strong and united. In *Our Wars with the Burmese*, Prince Damrong portrayed Siam fending off Burmese attacks for three hundred years. During the 1930s fear of fascism, Luang Wichit Wathakan took stories from Damrong's book and turned them into nationalistic plays. In 1997, the financial crisis was described as a third *sia krung*, the shorthand for the Burmese destruction of Ayutthaya. The Bang Rachan story, the climax of Damrong's history, became Thailand's most successful film ever. The daily newspapers present Burma as a primitive neighbor attacking Thailand with millions of little pills.

Second, each time the leaders try to militarize society. In the 1910s, King Vajiravudh set up the Wild Tiger Corps and made civilians play at being soldiers. In the 1930s, Wichit Wathakan's plays and songs idealized the Thai as a martial race. Recently the stock TV dramas of teenage romance, family crisis, and ghosts have been swept aside by the uniformed action drama—tales about brave soldiers, rangers, and policemen defending Thailand from corruption, gangsters, and drugs. In the recent *Phet Tat Phet*, the channel's entire stable of beautiful boys and beautiful girls was mobilized to give this militarization a real mass feel. The channels' self-censorship of violence has disappeared. Only a couple of years ago, really violent scenes were rare. Now these uniform dramas expend a small war's requirement of ammunition in a single episode. In the title sequences, the body count is several per second.

Third, these tales of resistance feature the Woman Warrior. In the anti-colonial phase, these were fighting queens. In the old chronicles, Suriyothai got only a single line. By the time of Damrong's *Our Wars with the Burmese*, she had expanded to a full-length story. Now she is revived as a three-hour film epic.

In the 1930s, the new anti-absolutist leaders looked round for commoners in this role. Thao Suranaree of Khorat was rescued from the obscurity of a very brief, vague historical reference, and given a whole story and a statue. Now she too may find her way onto celluloid. But these revivals are self-conscious remakes. The interesting update of the Woman Warrior is on TV. For the last couple of years, the image of a very beautiful woman carrying a very big gun has appeared time and again. In one drama last year, the audience waited weeks to find out whether the beautiful, athletic, sharp-shooting, and strangely ascetic female police ranger would blow away the gangster who had killed her father. In another, three achingly beautiful couples spent months wandering around the jungle. Several times in each episode, the heroines (with some male help) blew away a pursuing army of gangsters with AK-47s, revolvers, and cross-bows.

The uniformed action dramas are strewn with these modern Woman Warriors. They dash around in ultra-tight athletic outfits, then somehow produce enormous guns from nowhere. Only a couple of years ago, an aspiring starlet had to learn horse-riding, tennis, and golf. Now she has to visit the police academy and learn how to heft a Colt.

Fourth, the threat of being gobbled up always produces a reactive movement to gobble up the neighbors. In the colonial era, Bangkok sent off armies and mapmakers to enclose as much territory as possible before the colonialists got there first. In the 1940s, Wichit Wathakan explained why Siam had to invade Kengtung, Laos, and Cambodia: "When the present war is over, there will be no small nations in the world; all will be merged into big ones. So we either become a Power or are swallowed up by some other Power." Last year, one of the businessmen who launched a "new nationalist" organization urged Thailand to exploit the economies of Burma, Laos, and Cambodia so Thailand would be strong enough to fend off globalization. The new airport has been renamed from "cobra swamp" to Suvarnabhumi (golden land), the shorthand for this regional domination.

Fifth, these campaigns of resistance are used to justify strong leadership, but the qualifications of leadership change. Chulalongkorn and Vajiravudh opposed demands for democracy because of the need for unity against outside threats. They based their claim to leadership on tradition and absolutist right. In the 1930s, Phibun projected himself as *phunam*, the leader, explaining "The campaign is meant to demonstrate that we, the whole nation, can act as one person." Today, the old rhetoric of "unity" has become debased. Thaksin has subtly translated this into "Thais loving Thais." In this era of economic competition, his personal claim is based not on royal right or military command, but on money. He is businessman number one. In the Constitutional Court his nominal defense was that his female entourage made silly mistakes. But his real argument was that he has "so much money" that he is the right man to lead.

Sixth, there is a tell-tale metaphor which appears when these leadership claims come under attack. Vajiravudh reacted against democratic critics by imagining Siam as a small boat lost in a threatening sea: "Each person must decide whether to paddle and not argue with the helmsman, or jump out of the boat and swim." In the 1930s, Wichit Wathakan wrote: "The waters are treacherous; submerged rocks and whirlpools abound, deadly sharks swim freely. It is essential that we help each other and paddle as one."

In the current round, the paddle hasn't appeared yet. But look out for it later this year.[32]

---

32. It took a little longer than that, but it came: "Right now I am trying to steer the whole ship to the shoreline. Whether it's people I like, people who like me, or people who hate me, we're all trying to survive . . . Even those people I dislike, even if I wanted to kick them off the ship, I cannot. We must move together." (Thaksin quoted in *Bangkok Post*, 19 December 2003)

SPIK THAI NO CAN

4 August 2003

Uraiwan Thienthong, the minister of culture, is worried about the Thai language. Teenagers get grammar, syntax, and pronunciation wrong. The main problem is they use too many English words. Even teachers do this. The minister puts the blame firmly on the schools.

But really the problem is much broader than that. Kids have English words coming at them from all sides all the time. To understand the messages in just two ad-breaks last night, you needed to know these words: shampoo, body lotion, skin care, fast check, one two call, smooth, cyber shot, natural next step, whitening, yogurt, moisture, active, air, sexy, design, surround, heart, cream, purifying, foam, genius, and control. Only one ad (for instant noodles) was totally English-free.

The Ministry of Culture has set up language clinics in every province, and is planning to expand these to every district. The metaphor is intriguing. Poor language is a disease which can be cured by a doctor.

One of the minister's first patients would have to be her own boss, the prime minister. Sometimes, his condition seems to be chronic. He just cannot stop himself using English words. Here is a passage from a famous speech, with "e" showing an English word and "t" a Thai one:

e-t-t-t-e-t-t-t-e-t-t-t-t-e-e-e-t-t-t-t-t-t-e-e-t-t-t-t-t-t-e-e-e-e-e-
e-e-t-t-t-t-t-t-t-t-t-t-t-t-t-t-t-t-t-t-t-e-e-t-t-e-e-e-t-t-t-e-e-e-e-e-t-t-t-
e-e-t-t-t-t-t-t-t-t-t-t-e-e-e-e-e-t-t-t-e-t-t-e-t-t-e-e-e-t-t-t-t-t-t-e-t-t-t-t-
t-t-t-t-t-t-t-t-t-e-e-t-t-e

This was a speech on technology, so some of the English words were technical terms. But others were catchphrases which have perfectly good Thai equivalents. And some were fairly simple words: organization, commercial sense, convert, Indian, work, consumer, speed.

Thaksin is quite capable of speaking continuous Thai. In other speeches he scarcely uses a single foreign word. But he obviously likes to use lots of English. Just listen to his news sound bites and his radio talks. He regularly uses simple English words (sell, think, develop) which he could just as easily have spoken in Thai. It is part of his image as a modern, international, technological man. Possibly he also thinks he is helping to educate people, getting them more used to hearing foreign words, provoking them to learn what they mean.

The king has been a strong supporter of efforts to preserve and promote Thai. He uses English sparingly but with great effect. In his birthday speech last year, he described his now-famous dog as "mid-road." This is not a common adjective for dogs in English. In fact it might be unknown in this context. The phrase works because it is a literal translation from the Thai. The result is witty and endearing, a joke shared between speaker and audience, and very memorable.

But perhaps trying to erect walls around the Thai language is a denial or misunderstanding of the language's special character. All languages change all the time. Thai has been especially good at absorbing things from other languages.

This started long ago when Thai people and Khmer people were living mixed up together. The Thai language absorbed a lot from Khmer. This included a lot of fancy words which had originally come from the Indian languages of Pali and Sanskrit. Thai also borrowed from Khmer many simple words like walking, being born, or planting rice. To construct more complex sentences, Thai absorbed very basic words like: for, or, can, by, because, may. To construct more complex words, it borrowed principles for adding prefixes and suffixes.

So anyone now speaking Standard Thai is actually speaking a lot of Khmer. If someone from Chiang Mai goes somewhere where they speak another Tai-family language like Shan, Lao, Ahom, or Zhuang, it takes only a little time before the two sides can understand one another, because they both speak a fairly pure Tai language. But take a Bangkok speaker to these places, and there is complete mutual incomprehension.

Not only Khmer has been mixed into "Standard Thai," but also Mon,

Chinese, and much else. Take the first paragraph of the Draft Master-plan of Uraiwan's Ministry of Culture. If T means a Thai word, P is Pali, S is Sanskrit, and K is Khmer, this paragraph runs as follows:

T-T-K-T-P-P-T-S-T-T-P-T-K-T-S-T-K-K-T-K-P-T-P-K-T-T-T-T-T-T-
P-T-P-T-T-T-T-K-T-P-T-T-T-K-T-K-T-T-T-T-K-T-K-T-P-T-T-T-T-K-
T-T-T-S-T-T-T-T-T-T-T-T-T-T-T-K-T-K-T-P-K-T-T-K-T-S-P-T-K-
T-K-T-S-T-T-T-T-P-T-T-T-T-P-T-T-T-K-K-T-P-T-T-K-T-P-K-T-K-T-
T-K-T-T-K-T-P

About half the words have been adopted from other languages (probably more, but Chang Noi is not an expert). All these words are of course now "Thai." The point is that Thai has been very successful in absorbing from other languages. The great administrator and scholar, Prince Damrong, reckoned this absorbent quality was one reason why Thai had been so successful as a language, society, and culture through history.

Language is a social tool. When society changes, language changes too. In this globalization age, the boundaries of language are bound to be breached. Between Uraiwan and Thaksin, there seem to be two different strategies for dealing with this, and they reflect different versions of nationalism.

Uraiwan's strategy seems to be to set up a language Border Patrol Police to hold back the English invasions. Last week, the Ministry of Culture ran a campaign on preserving the Thai language under the title: Love the country, revere the culture, cherish the language. Somehow, this sort of nationalism loves this kind of triplet.

But Thaksin does not seem so interested in the old nationalism which is all about unity and tradition. In a fascinating aside a few weeks ago, he wondered aloud whether Thai nationalism focused too much on symbols (the flag was his example, but language would be another), rather than realities. He had just returned from the US. At a guess, he was impressed how countries like the US (and most Western nations) manipulate nationalism for advantage in the international arena. In other words, an outward nationalism not an inward one. Following his logic, Thais need to be patriotic, but they also need to know English.

Building a fortress round the language is not a good idea. If Thai had been resolutely defended down through the ages, then the minister of culture, Uraiwan Thienthong, would not exist (as it were), since her name is Sanskrit-Chinese-Mon.

INCONVENIENT TRUTHS OF CENSORSHIP UNDER GLOBALIZATION

16 April 2007

Censorship is nearly always a form of denial, an attempt to hide a truth or limit its power. If someone wants to write or shout something quite meaningless or uninteresting, then nobody takes much notice anyway. Censors reach for the blue pencil, the scissors, and the off-switch when there really is something that most people want to know and a few people want to hide.

Every Thai government gets the urge to censor. In the political culture, there is a memory of the good times (for governments) when they could stop most criticism by one means or another. But over the past three decades, suppression has become more and more difficult. There is a growing audience of people who want to know what is going on, and hence an expanding business opportunity in supplying that demand. Even if government controls the mainstream electronic media and can heavy the press, there are other channels. Way back, the popular method was leaflets. Then came faxes. Then SMS messaging and community radio. And now email, blogs, and websites. This sequence has an important feature: the old forms were local, the new ones are global.

But censorship is not what it used to be. Consider the case of the royal biography which was banned in Thailand before the book's publication in the US last year. Despite the ban, photocopied versions circulated widely in Thailand even before the publication date. Purchase through online booksellers has not been too difficult. Parts of the book have been scanned and placed on the web. Passages have been translated into Thai and also placed on the web or circulated in other ways. Cheap illegal photocopied version have been on sale furtively in the city. The content of the book has been widely discussed in web forums.

This book is expensive, heavy, and in English. Normally the readership of such a tome would be limited to those who have the money to buy it, the language skills to understand it, and the commitment to wade through it. Censorship often tends to raise a book's notoriety and hence its attraction. But in the new world of more open media, a ban can also increase a book's readership by making it cheaper and more widely accessible.

Such censorship no longer achieves its supposed purpose of actually preventing people from gaining access to the information being provided. Rather such censorship is just a public statement of disapproval. Official authorities still seem to think they have to issue such statements of disapproval, perhaps because they are reluctant to admit that their power has diminished in practice. But such censorship can become a form of viral marketing which both advertises a product and expands its distribution channels.

The YouTube affair[33] has followed the same pattern, with some added features. The attempt to suppress the first video posted on the site only gave birth to at least seven more. The wholesale blocking of the YouTube site in Thailand spawned a cottage industry for devising work-arounds and other forms of distribution. The prominence given to the issue in the press meant that the numbers who knew about the videos and who had a chance to see them multiplied many times beyond the few who regularly trawl YouTube.

In the international arena, the impact of the Thai official protests were even more virulent. Every day, hundreds of clips are posted on YouTube but only a small fraction gain the kind of publicity and notoriety of this batch. The protests by the Thai government ran as major stories on CNN and BBC World, and appeared on the front pages of several international newspapers. Undoubtedly this boosted the numbers who viewed the videos around the world far above the average for a YouTube clip. Through these stories, many more people got to know about the Oliver Jufer[34] case, the existence in Thailand of a lese majeste

---

33. A forty-four-second video with graffiti superimposed on the face of the king was placed on YouTube. Several similar clips followed. In response, government blocked access to YouTube from April to August 2007.

34. A Swiss national convicted in March 2007 of lese majeste for drunkenly spraying

law, and the enthusiasm of Thai authorities for imposing censorship. These international media stories were usually scrupulous in pointing out that many people in Thailand found the videos very offensive because of widespread reverence for the king. Yet as a whole these stories portrayed Thailand as a government struggling to impose its own repressive habits on the world.

Internally, however, the YouTube affair has been a massive success for the junta. Various government figures proclaimed that the clips were an attempt to undermine the monarchy, an attack on Thailand as a country, or a threat to national security. Of course, the clips were none of these things. They were very specifically protests over the Jufer case, which many people feel strongly is a legitimate object of protest (whether or not you agree with the sentiment or the method).

Many journalists and commentators, who would normally think of themselves as defenders of free expression in the face of censorship, joined the chorus calling for YouTube to censor the videos, and lambasting YouTube spokespersons for defending the principle of free speech. Some of these journalists and commentators have been highly critical of government censorship over past months, and had professed outrage at the closure of the Rajdamnoen Room chat site hosted by the pantip.com site, one of the most popular and active political discussion sites in Thailand.

You could imagine the government censors grinning with glee. Here were some of their major critics lining up to call for censorship.

The people who have been put in the most difficult position over this affair are the Thai journalists, academics, commentators, and activists who truly support the principle of free expression. It has been almost impossible for them to come out against the call for YouTube to be censored. They would lay themselves wide open to be pilloried as anti-monarchist by those who like to act more royalist than the institution. Wisely they have kept quiet. But this has consolidated this incident as an enormous success for the junta in winning support for the principle of censorship.

---

paint on posters of the king. He was given a pardon by the king and deported.

CULTURAL BUREAUCRACY AND BUREAUCRATIC CULTURE

12 November 2007

A television ad aired a couple of years ago showed a youth whose back, when tapped, resounded with a loud boinggg. This was supposed to be funny, and there was even a bit of canned laughter after every boinggg to make sure the viewer understood that. The intended message was that the lad's back was so stiff he could not assume a correct pose of stooping deference. The ad was made by the Ministry of Culture.

The ministry has recently reissued a booklet entitled "Thai Social Etiquette."[35] The booklet is written in English and offers visiting foreigners the usual tips about making a proper *wai*, not pointing with the feet, and not patting the head. But it is much more wide-ranging than most such guides. It tells its readers how to sit, eat, lie down, walk, speak, dress, make a phone call, queue for the loo, drink, use a spoon, give a speech, pay a visit, and perform at a seminar.

It is not really a handbook on how foreigners should behave in Thailand, but rather a manual on how Thais should behave in their own country. It sums it all up like this:

"In Thai society, where seniority is given much importance and politeness to everyone is stressed, in order to be a person with good manners, one must be aware and careful of almost every gesture or movement, and also of almost every word or sentence one utters."

Let's imagine a newly arrived foreigner toting this book along to some of the common everyday spaces in Thai society. At the open-air restaurant, she would find that most of the booklet's rules (not reaching across, always using a serving spoon, making sure to wipe lipstick off your glass) were being broken at almost every table. The lively

---

35. The booklet is available at: http://www.m-culture.go.th/culture01/culture01-uploads/libs/document/b0773f58d1.pdf

atmosphere would make her doubt that all the people present were being careful with their every gesture and their every word.

In a business office or factory, the foreigner would find people interacting without any attention to the booklet's rules about social behavior. In a village, all the booklet's procedures about how to pay a social call would make no sense at all. In the shopping mall, bus, or Skytrain, the visitor would be forced to conclude that almost none of the people were Thai since they did not seem to walk, talk, sit, or dress in the prescribed manner. The booklet warns, "Refrain from holding hands in public as it may have undesirable implication," and declares that "Men do not roll up their sleeves as if getting ready for a fight," but the visitor would find even such desperately stern injunctions being transgressed in full public view.

By now the visitor might conclude that the booklet is a work of complete fantasy on the level of *Star Wars*. But that would be wrong. The society described and idealized in the booklet does exist, but is not "Thai society," either past or present. Rather it is one rarefied segment of the society, occupied by senior bureaucrats of the sort that work in or with the Ministry of Culture.

They have some defining characteristics. They have a good surname proving they come from a good family—or else they wish they did. They have a private income because it is difficult to maintain the proper public display on the standard bureaucratic pittance—or at least they wish they did. They belong to a profession which used to be very influential but which is being rapidly marginalized as the society becomes richer, more commercial, and more open—and they have nostalgia for an idealized past.

If you remove from the etiquette booklet all the advice which is really universal (e.g., don't eat with your mouth open), it has one clear message: hierarchy is everything, and deference is always due.

Since its reincarnation in the early 2000s, the Ministry of Culture has had two main roles. First, it administers a small budget to preserve and promote valuable creative work, past and present. This is Culture with a capital C, and is a very valid and necessary role.

But the Ministry of Culture also wants to be the Ministry of culture with a small c. This is dangerous because "culture" is such a slippery word. Does it mean how people actually live? Or how some people think other people ought to live?

In the early years after its rebirth, the ministry spent a lot of effort compiling a masterplan defining its role. The first part of this plan goes out of its way to emphasize how varied Thai society is (in ethnicity, region, urban/rural, occupation), and how dynamic it is as part of the modern globe. This part is descriptive—describing how things are in all their messy variety. But moving to the second part which frames what the ministry is going to do, the plan slips into another mode altogether. This part is prescriptive— prescribing how things ought to be. And this part junks the enthusiasm for messy variety in favor of a much narrower view.

The results have been both hilarious and tragic. The ministry has tried to outlaw risqué songs on the grounds that they are "against Thai culture" when in fact these songs belong to a great tradition of boisterous counterpoint singing which is the historical culture of far more Thais than the courtly arts. The ministry rages against "un-Thai" forms of dress which are rather similar to the way most ordinary people dressed around a century ago. Much more tragically, the ministry has obstructed some highly creative contemporary work in theater, cinema, and the plastic arts.

In these obstructive actions, as in the boingg-back ad and the etiquette booklet, the ministry claims a right and duty to impose the values of a declining minority on the society as a whole. Perhaps the ministry should obey one of the rules from its own etiquette booklet: "Do not scratch here and scratch there."

THAI STUDIES AND THE MONARCHY

22 January 2008

In early January, some four hundred scholars from around the world met in Bangkok for the 10th International Conference on Thai Studies. This academic jamboree takes place every three years. All the usual subjects were on the agenda—Buddhism, weaving, democracy, the history of Ayutthaya, agrarian relations, and Thai arts. But there was also something new and different. Three panels were devoted to discussion of the monarchy. Another two focused on the Sufficiency Economy. And more papers on monarchical topics were scattered around other sessions. Never before has this subject attracted such attention.

Of course, it is odd to have any serious discussion of Thailand past and present without factoring in the monarchy. At previous conferences, the matter has been treated gingerly out of a mixture of deference and fear of legal complications. But the public presence of the monarchy in the life of the nation has expanded steadily over past decades. This is partly the result of the current long and remarkable reign, as reflected in the two massive celebrations of the 60th jubilee and 80th birthday over recent months. It is partly because the idea of the Sufficiency Economy has been placed in the public domain and vigorously promoted as a guide for policymaking that will affect everybody. And it is partly because some figures closely associated with the monarchic institution have had prominent roles in the tense political conflict of the past two years. More and more, the monarchy has become a subject that is impossible to leave out.

But this is still a delicate matter, especially for a meeting held inside Thailand. The organizers came under some pressure over the issue. To their credit, the host institution, Thammasat University, went ahead on grounds that these were legitimate subjects for academic discussion. Still, Special Branch officers attended the sessions (at one point, a floor speaker cheekily suggested they should be thanked for their presence), and one chief organizer was interviewed by police until late at night.

The first monarchy panel analyzed some things which have created the special character of the current reign. One panelist looked at the unique popular image of the monarch as a Buddhist king, a source of progress and well-being, and as a guide in the difficult and dangerous transition to modernity. A second panelist told how the financial foundations of the monarchy were laid a century ago. These investments had a rocky ride in the 1997 financial crisis but had ultimately emerged stronger through careful restructuring. A third panelist traced the development of the Privy Council over sixty years. This advisory body began as a group of mainly royal family members, but expanded into a mixture of security experts, development technocrats, and jurists, reflecting the breadth of the institution's interests. A related paper in another panel examined how the Royal Projects had helped to mold a "mass consciousness" about the nature of the monarchy, and to influence the direction of national policies.

A second panel focused on the lese majeste law. A legal expert traced the history of the law, showing how its scope had widened over time. A journalist demonstrated how the media played safe and practiced self-censorship, resulting in much more restrictive coverage than that required by law.

In the panels on the Sufficiency Economy, speakers wondered whether the thinking was relevant given the extent to which livelihoods had changed over the past generation, and given the evident enthusiasm for embracing capitalism at all levels of the society.

Collectively, these various contributions demonstrated the immense complexity of the institution. In image, the monarchy is both a traditional Buddhist kingship and a pioneer of modernity. Through its investments, the crown is at the center of Thailand's growing capitalist economy, while royal theories on development seem designed to shield ordinary people from the same process. The developments over sixty years in law, public image, and institutions like the Privy Council reflect major changes in the meaning of monarchy.

By laying out this complexity, the conference panels quietly made a case for the need to understand the institution better. And through the conduct of the panels, this was shown to be possible. There was no shallow opinionation, no grinding of axes, no flashy posturing. Most of the papers displayed weighty research, balanced argument, and subtle use of language.

At the last of the panels, four very distinguished scholars offered their reactions to Paul Handley's, *The King Never Smiles*. The room was packed, with people standing in every available space, and more in three overflow rooms. The panel was almost buried by the sweaty, airless crush. Even without a word spoken, the atmosphere told of the importance of this moment.

The first speaker said that the role of the monarchy had evidently changed from 1973 onwards, and the book was simply one attempt to catch up with the reality. The second thought the title was silly and the writer's assumptions often too American, but in the end it was a good book that could have been better. The third lamented that Handley seemed to think ritual and symbolism was "a silly idea," but welcomed that the book "challenges the agreement to silence, or the agreement not to disagree." The trouble with repression is that "when silence is enforced for a long time, noise—when it comes—is deafening."

The fourth speaker asked the simple question, "What is all the fuss about?" There were many Thais discussing and analyzing the monarchy, as the conference sessions had shown. Possibly, the panic over the book arose because the author was a foreign journalist, rather than an academic. Banning had been ineffective. Chapters were available in translation on the web. When asked if they had read the book, many Thais present raised their hands. What would happen, the speaker asked, if the book was translated and published in Thai? Possibly, he suggested, people would find the content so familiar and unremarkable that it would be dismissed as "Nothing new. Ordinary stuff."

Birds, bees, and beasts

1999—THE YEAR OF THE BODY

8 December 1999

1999 has been the year of the body. Mostly Luk-Ket's body. And most of Luk-Ket's body.

Some months ago, Methinee (Luk-Ket) Kingphayom appeared on a magazine cover clad in angel wings and a very small amount of silver foil. A few weeks ago, she was draped across the full width of *Thai Rath*'s front page wearing only a stick-on tattoo. Last week she graced the same front page, languorously teamed up with Pathumrat (Helen) Woramali and no visible sign of clothing.

Thai Rath's front page is arguably the most public place in the kingdom. Half the urban population pays a visit every day. This page has always given its readers an occasional *malai* (garland) of a pretty girl. But over this year, the shots have become noticeably bolder. This is part of a trend. There are more and more magazines (like *M*) targeting male readers with risky cover shots. The underwear ads decorating Bangkok's bus shelters have adopted more of the soft-porn techniques of multiple images, headless torsos, and very young models looking vulnerable. The hit film *Nang Nak* spent much of its footage caressing the naked skin of its beautiful stars. The TV knockoff is repeating the technique in a toned-down version. *Matichon Weekly*, one of the leading current affairs magazines, has a regular column reviewing nude and semi-nude photographs. Its subjects include Luk-Ket and the usual starlets, but also society figures and Japanese schoolgirls. The prose is a mixture of art criticism and heavy breathing.

Something is changing—something about taste, ethics, and public acceptability. Does this mark a shift away from "traditional values"? Not really. There is a great local tradition of appreciating the female form. Many believe Thai court dances and dramas were performed so agonizingly slowly to give the audience time for a good inspection. The enthusiasm for beauty contests is a direct descent from this tradition. It's no surprise that the Miss Thailand contest has been run by the alumni association of Vajiravudh College, the Thai aristocracy's adaptation of an English public school. Flesh-watching is traditional. The *Thai Rath* front page is just a democratic adaptation.

But over recent decades, the growth of a big commercial sex industry on the one hand, and of a new middle class on the other, has seen a strict division between "good girls" and "bad girls." Bad girls do things for money. Good girls dress and behave in ways which ensure they can never be mistaken for bad girls. Codes of dress and behavior have been developed to enable good girls to distance themselves from bad.

These codes are complex. And changing. Exposing lots of flesh is something usually only bad girls would do. But girls who are so obviously good (as proved by their surname, behavior, track record) can show a lot and get away with it. Exposure is only one part of the equation—albeit a very important part.

So even deliberate acts of exposure like beauty contests can be good-girl affairs. Indeed, the organizers of the Miss Thailand contest worked hard to achieve a good-girl image. Winners are bound by strict rules of what they cannot do. Whether wearing bikinis was non-Thai was a deep and important issue that had to be aired and resolved by public debate. The event is staged with lashings of prestige and decorum.

For young female entertainers, the dividing line between good and bad is especially tricky. They are expected to be sexy. But they risk disaster if they cross an invisible line. A few years ago, risky pictures of the singer Mai Charoenpura appeared on the *Thai Rath* front page. She was converted instantly from good girl to bad. Stories started to circulate about her bad love life. For months afterwards, the rumor-mill spotted her disporting herself in bad-girl ways. She had to disappear from sight, and reappear dressed in white singing soppy songs to earn her rehabilitation.

Recently Dawan Singwi became a bad girl overnight. Nobody found anything wrong with her displaying herself in student beauty contests. But when her pictures appeared in *M* magazine, all hell broke loose. The pictures were significantly less erotic than an average bus shelter ad. But she was roundly condemned, almost denied her university degree, and obliged to perform instant penance in rueful TV interviews.

The two cases show the complexity of the code. Actresses, models, and beauty-contestants display their bodies as a profession. In these professional roles, the rules are different. But Mai is a singer. Apart from the fact that the pictures were a little over-bold for the time, there was no good reason for a singer to be so revealing. In Dawan's case, she was still technically a student. Taking part in a university beauty contest was okay. It was amateur and internal. Selling the pictures to *M* magazine was not okay. It was commercial and public. Most agreed that a month later when she had ceased to be a student, the pictures would have caused no stir. The distinction is subtle and Dawan herself looked genuinely bewildered at the furor. She had threatened to undermine the special magic associated with higher education.

The Mai and Dawan cases help to define the boundary between what good girls and bad girls can display. Luk-Ket is moving those boundaries. She is primarily a model and thus a professional in self-display. She also dresses like a million dollars and behaves without blemish. It is impossible to mistake her for a bad girl. But then she also appears a lot on TV dramas and game shows. She has acquired the kind of girl-next-door familiarity which attaches to those people who enter our homes every night through the silver screen. She appears in wholesome and educational family entertainment in the evening, and reappears pouting nakedly out of *Thai Rath*'s front page next morning.

Moreover, Luk-Ket's latest appearance with Helen is a deliberate move into bad-girl territory. In fact, a takeover bid. Girly calendars are a year-end tradition. The most famous in the past were produced by tire companies and liquor brands. They deliberately gave an exciting bad-girl image. Recently Mekong whisky announced it would stop producing its famous girly calendars on grounds such bad-girl stuff seemed out-of-date. Luk-Ket and Helen have seen the gap in the market. They are producing their own calendar. By the time this piece appears, its 30,000 copies will have sold out in nanoseconds.

How can they invade this bad-girl territory and still stay good? Maybe three reasons. First, they are presenting themselves not as poor victims of commercial exploitation, but as sharp entrepreneurs. The calendar, we are told, is their own joint investment. Second, their calendar will be more "modern" than the Mekong predecessors. Proof is the fact that it will be featured on the hallmark of modernity, its own website.

Third, they tell us the calendar is a service to the nation and Thai womanhood. Helen said to *Thai Rath*: "We decided to bring out this sexy calendar to raise Thai modeling to world standards. Thai models are no less beautiful than international ones. Besides Luk-Ket and I both have the Miss Thailand World title as a guarantee. We want to help Thai girls to dare come out and show themselves, to be in control of their own lives, and have more confidence in themselves." By coincidence, the *Matichon* nude columnist ran a piece on Helen in the same week. After slavering over various parts of her body, he commented that "her aggressive nose shows she is clever."

Thai feminism has paid little attention to exploitation of the female image. After all, there have been more direct forms of female exploitation to think about. But when the good girl from the game show can take off her clothes repeatedly in the most public space in the kingdom, something is changing. Is this, as Helen claims, just two girls making their independent way in the world, and striking a blow for nation and woman? Or is it opening up a new area of female exploitation?

WELCOME TO THIGHLANDIA, LANNAWORLD, AND SPLATKRAN

30 April 2001

When the Thai economy hits trouble, the government turns to tourism. It happened in the last crisis in the early 1980s. With agriculture slumping and industry moribund, the economic planners seized on services. They sent two hundred thousand Thai workers off to the Middle East, and doubled tourist arrivals in five years.

As the prime minister said a few days ago, tourism is quick, cheap, and easy. The ingredients are already there. Sun, sea, sand, smiles, culture. Some of these spare resources haven't even been sold yet. With better marketing, the returns will jump. Twenty billion baht more from Chiang Mai. Ten more from Phuket. And another twenty from everywhere else. All by this time next year.

Amid this enthusiasm, it's difficult to detect words like "control" or "consequences."

The consequences are not a matter of theory or prediction. The evidence is there for anyone who wants to look. Thailand's main tourist product is the beach resort, with sea, sun, sand, and the other S-word which the tourist planners seem so reluctant to talk about. The development cycle is clear from the experience of forty years.

Stage 1. Start with a place of outstanding beauty that attracts people because it is drop-dead gorgeous. Impose absolutely no controls. Allow get-rich-quick entrepreneurs to encroach on the beach, blow up the rocks, scatter garbage, and pour concrete everywhere.

Stage 2. The resort is now popular but rapidly losing its natural charm. Add large quantities of sex and comfort. Build large luxurious hotels. Import lots of girls.

Stage 3. By now the natural beauty is totally obliterated. The seafront is an essay in bad architecture. The hinterland is a shanty town of beer bars. Develop the remains as a male fantasy theme park. Add anything with testosterone appeal—big motorbikes, shooting ranges, go-kart tracks, boxing rings, archery. Bring in more and more girls (and boys, and children). There you have it: Thighlandia. Then stack it high and sell it cheap.

You can travel round Thailand and see this development cycle in action. Pattaya is long into stage 3. It is very, very hard to imagine that thirty years ago Pattaya was a series of pretty bays of astounding beauty. Phuket is hovering on the borderline between stage 2 and stage 3. The island has become a building site. Patong is spreading like a stain. The hills behind the beaches are being systematically concreted over with hotels and apartments. The interior is filling up with all the testosterone stuff—shooting ranges, go-kart tracks, big bikes.

Hua Hin is on the edge between stage 1 and stage 2. The architectural assault on the beauty of the beachfront is complete. Over the last year, Patong-ization has started, and the old fishing village is filling up with girls, bars, and the trappings of Thighlandia.

Thailand's second tourist product is the hill town offering a mixture of mountain scenery, old culture, and exotic peoples. This also has its own development cycle. The first visitors are attracted by nature and adventure. They climb the hills, paddle the rivers, visit the hill peoples, experience the temples. They generate little revenue, but they create a reputation. At stage 2, people arrive who want to experience the place, but also want to buy some of it and take it home. A temple carving. A hilltribe necklace. A video of the elephant ride.

As the numbers of visitors increase, the original appeal of nature and adventure is swamped. The temples are buried by high-rise hotels. The treks are too crowded to offer any fantasy of adventure. What's left is selling things to take home. At stage 3, the place is transformed into an exotic theme park with a huge specialty store. The hill peoples and other "natural" attractions are arranged like a zoo. The "traditional native products" are manufactured on industrial principles, and sold through an ever-spreading flea market. Then add some of the bits of Thighlandia for good measure. Welcome to LannaWorld.

Thailand's third tourist product is the festival. Mostly these have been marketed domestically. But in the last few years, the tourist authority has started turning these into export products.

Originally Songkran was a subtle mix of two festivals found all over Asia. The first is an intimate rite of blessing by pouring water. The second is the world-turned-upside-down. For one day only, the hierarchy is upended, and social constraints are removed. Both these festivals have cultural meaning and social purpose. The rite of blessing brings people together. The day-of-misrule is an opportunity to release tensions and adjust hierarchies.

Songkran today has become a water fight. It's exhilarating and great fun. But in essence it's a blown-up version of a paintball battle, a real world experience of a videogame splatfest. The underlying principle (as with battle simulations and arcade wars) is the exercise of violence (bang, bang), relieved of all its nasty consequences (blood and death). The rite of blessing has disappeared. The drama of misrule has been lost. Welcome to Splatkran.

The current enthusiasm for tourism is more than Thaksin's dream of a quick fix in a bad year, a *ya ba* pill for the economy. Last year, the World Bank produced a report on Thailand's economic prospects after the crisis. Shorn of all the formal language, the report said: everything else is hopeless, turn Thailand into a theme park. Recently the tourist authority announced its ambition to raise tourist arrivals to 20 million people in this decade. Over the last twenty years, the number has risen from 1 million to 9.6 million. The proposal now is to double that in a handful of years. That means another Pattaya, another Phuket, another Patong, another battered "Rose of the North," another Splatkran.

Realistically, this has gone too far to stop. But since the consequences are so easy to see, some controls might seem sensible. Or else the Tourist Authority might have to change its current domestic slogan, from "Go, or you won't know," to "Go, or it won't be there."

SOCIAL ORDER, MORAL PANIC, AND NAVELS

4 March 2002

In all the polls on the Thaksin government's first year, Purachai Pium-sombun scores higher recognition than anyone other than the prime minister. Yet a year ago, few had heard of him. In the polls, his "social order" campaign gained the highest approval ratings. Yet a year ago, the idea of such a campaign had never been publicly discussed. Why have Purachai and "social order" touched such a chord?

Probably because "social order" responds to two forms of moral panic that have risen sharply over the last few years.

The first is the fear of the wild. The urban middle class has been struggling to build a secure world, governed by rules and laws, where things are predictable and reasonable. The economic boom gave them the means to invest in a new lifestyle. Political liberalization brought a new constitution and new laws which enshrine their aspirations. But this urban middle-class world seems like a clearing in the jungle. Beyond the borders are the wilds, populated by godfathers, tricky businessmen, and powerful people who think they can get away with anything.

Since the 1997 financial crisis, the fear of the wild has increased. The modern economy, whose expansion was the motor of growing middle-class aspirations, has been pole-axed. The informal, invisible, or illegal economy is growing. This is obvious from the statistics. All the indicators of growth in the formal economy (exports, investment, government spending) are negative or neutral. Yet GDP is somehow growing at 2 percent. The difference must be underground. The meth-amphetamine boom is the most obvious evidence. Gambling is on a roll. Oil smuggling may be undergoing a revival. Moreover, the press reports on these activities consistently show that people in uniform play a major role. Of course they are a small minority. But over the last decade, they have displaced many competitors because of their unique comparative advantages.

The impact is very real. Methamphetamines have escaped from the slums and entered the mainstream schools where the best market are the middle class kids with some money in their pocket. The night entertainment industry, around which much of the underground economy revolves, has escaped from its traditional zones and spread like a stain into commercial and residential areas.

The second moral panic is about sex. There has been a sharp, generational shift in attitudes and practices over the last few years. The new generation starts younger. They do it more casually. They often do it more carelessly, too. Sexual explicitness has risen in the public culture. Nice girls who model or act now take off their clothes for the front pages of the daily papers and glossy magazines. Television dramas are fascinated with violent rape. Teenage fashion has become aggressively sexy. Shoulders emerge under spaghetti straps. Navels peep out from the gap between the falling waist-line and the shrinking tank-top.

This generational shift has prompted a series of mini-panics. About models who are role-models moving into the nude calendar game. About students selling sex. About Siam Hotel becoming an open-access flesh market. About Siam Square and Royal City Avenue. About sex education materials that might really educate.

Where these two themes of moral panic converge is in the night market, in the night entertainment industry. Good girls mix with bad girls. Good girls dress like bad girls. Good girls may even act like bad girls. Who can tell the difference? Who can find the dividing line any more?

There's a striking vignette in Coke's recent ad. The teenage heroine goes to a Kat concert. She is whipped into a frenzy by eye-contact identification with her singer idol, and by the intensity of sound and movement conveyed by a quick-cut sequence visually dominated by the image of Kat's exposed and pulsing navel. Mum picks her up afterwards and asks how the concert was. The heroine starts opening her mouth at high excitement level but then transits instantly to the adult-populated world, kills her rapture, and shrugs "so-so." Even laced with Coke's sticky sweetness, this is a moral tale about the wild and the tame.

The night market is where the young middle class come as consumers, the underground as producers and vendors, and the dodgy men in uniform as tax collectors and protectors. It is where the tame rubs shoulders with the wild.

By imposing some limits and some rules on the night market, Purachai is responding to these two themes of moral panic. But, so what? Is he merely treating some minor symptoms rather than the real disease? Particularly in the case of the expanding illegal economy, is there not a larger problem over law, enforcement, and the police?

Certainly. But there is also a practical issue over how to approach this bigger problem. Frontal attempts to kickstart police reform have got nowhere. The public may want reform but is too resigned to agitate for it. Without popular pressure, the politicians see no gain, only risk. Even public scandalization, like the candid camera exposure of police corruption, is only a short-term news story.

But Purachai's actions are new and unpredictable. When the cue ball slams into the pack, other balls bounce and cannon in all directions. Already, Purachai's actions are having three consequences. First, in Khon Kaen, the police and military have begun a war of mutual accusations over one another's protection rackets. The large sums and the police/military involvement have been detailed in press reports and academic research. But it is rare to have confirmation from such authoritative sources. Second, some police stations are said to be facing fiscal crisis because of the decline of their night market income. Third, the impact of the campaign on both protectors and entrepreneurs is being translated into political pressure to have Purachai stopped. And that pressure opens up the rift between reformism and gangsterism that runs right through Thai Rak Thai.[36]

Social order is as provocative as a pulsing navel.

---

36. Purachai was moved from Interior to Justice in a reshuffle on 3 October 2002, and then made a deputy prime minister overseeing health from 8 February 2003. In essence, he was sidelined because his ethical approach conflicted with the internal working of the government itself. In January 2005, he quit politics and went to live in New Zealand.

SEX BOMB, SEX BOMB . . .

2 September 2003

The sprawling sex trade shelters under a simple and creative hypocrisy. Peddling prostitution is technically illegal, but everyone knows that the big glitzy buildings alongside the office towers, hospitals, and government agencies are selling the world's oldest product.

The law makes this possible. Prostitution can be charged only if the guilty are caught in the act. Police would have to burst through the door of the massage parlor and find the client busily engaged while simultaneously handing payment to the parlor owner with a spare hand. Surveys have shown that the police consider prostitution an unimportant matter and make no effort to enforce the laws. To salvage some semblance of moral authority, they claim to crackdown on the nastier margins of the sex trade—under-age girls, use of force to coerce girls against their will, and the horrified discovery that girls undergoing the blessing of education are tempted to earn money this way.

For some time, this seemed to be a stable situation. Mum and dad drove the kids past all these huge, strangely blind buildings to school where they were taught in social ethics class that the family is the sacrosanct core of Thai society. Authorities, without irony, cracked down on bare nipples, spaghetti straps, and songs about flabby buttocks on grounds such things are too sexy for "social order" and "Thai culture." The minister enforcing "social order" confessed he used to visit massage parlors, but gave it up before taking up his new job.[37] The blank walls of the massage parlors were enough to divide reality from imagination.

Chuwit Kamolwisit is a sex bomb that has blown up this stable state. He began doing so long before his current reincarnation as a political satirist and public clown. He went to business school and then applied

---

37. Pracha Maleenont, who became a deputy interior minister in October 2002, said he had given up frequenting massage parlors "a long time ago."

the principles of integration, scale, advertising, and promotion to the sex industry. The pimp's role in the sex trade is simply to bring the demand to meet the supply. But what differentiates suppliers is the packaging of the foreplay. Three varieties are popular: dalliance in a cocktail lounge, crooning karaoke, or a soapy pummeling in a bathtub. Following the principles of modern mega-retail, Chuwit integrated these three in a single outlet with sufficient scale to cater for a range of consumer tastes. He replaced the somewhat subdued promotional strategies of older outlets (flashing lights, slightly risqué names) with giant blow-ups of gorgeous, realistic, and enticing girls. The parlor walls were no longer much of a barrier because Chuwit invited the passer-by to imagine the inside.

From that point, his rise to notoriety was only a matter of time. But taking the walls off the massage parlors is revealing a lot more than bath tubs.

First, Chuwit is using the television channels, owned by this government committed to social order and Thai culture, to offer public education on the economics of sex commerce. In a TV interview, he described how he single-mindedly wasted his time in educational institutions, and then made a million baht a day once he entered the sex business. Ambitious students were presumably taking detailed notes. He has encouraged his workers to tell us they retain 1,200 baht a session, and might manage three to five sessions a day. Any village girl with elementary school maths can work out that in a few months she can make her parents' lifetime earnings from hardscrabble paddy farming. That should boost the supply of workers.

The press has done its bit for demand. One weekly news magazine launched a series of personal memoirs of the parlor, written as over-the-top war stories. Slightly tongue-in-cheek, they claim the parlors have become a necessary balm for the stress of living in Bangkok. Chuwit is already claiming he is a "social welfarist" for providing employment to destitute girls. These articles make him a "social therapist" for providing recuperative services to devastated men. This should boost the customer demand.

Second, the ambiguous position of the sex trade as illegal-but-allowed enables the police to levy huge amounts of informal tax. A parlor pays an initial fee for its "license" to do business, and then monthly taxes roughly computed on turnover. Payments are both in cash and kind. There are extra fees for security services. What happened in the destruction of the Sukumwit Soi 10 is no longer in dispute.[38] The bars were smashed. Various uniformed groups were involved. According to one version, Chuwit ordered the services and paid for them. According to the other version, the groups carried out the operation in the spirit of private enterprise and then blackmailed Chuwit to pay for it. The difference between the two versions is only a little detail over the invoicing.

Third, how come this Chuwit show is playing on our TV screens and newspaper pages for week after week? Credit is due to Chuwit for the continuous creativity he has brought to the performance. But it seems likely that a show of this kind needs a special license to continue so long. Speculation has been rife. Many are convinced that Chuwit is godfathered from high up. The prime minister may get the chance to replace a police chief he has never seemed happy with. He may put his police classmates and friends in positions vacated after Chuwit's revelations. He may be happy for us to be distracted by the Chuwit show, rather than worrying about the terrorism decree, or the stock market being entrusted to someone deeply entwined in Thailand's worst-ever bank crash, or the crumbling of the public health system, or whatever.

Bangkok mums and dads can still drive the kids to school past those funny buildings. But now they have to squeeze their eyes tighter shut to avoid seeing the pimp entrepreneurs, crooked cops, mafia enforcers, and opportunistic politicians behind their walls.

---

38. Chuwit had bought the plot for 500 million baht, but it was occupied by vendors, makeshift bars, and other small businesses. On the night of 26 January 2003, around four hundred people invaded the site, smashed up everything, and leveled the ground with a grader by morning. A superb story on Chuwit ran in the *Guardian Weekly*, see www.guardian.co.uk/weekend/story/0,3605,1151521,00.html

THE NIPPLE CRISIS

24 November 2003

The fashion show was meant to be spectacular, and the dress designed to be daring. That one of Methinee Luk-Ket's breasts slipped out was, well, simple physics. The photographers did their job: they snapped it. The sensationalist press did its job: it sensationalized it. Now the Ministry of Culture wants to send police to fashion shows and tighten up legislation to prevent repetition of such "un-Thai" behavior.

Drafting the legislation, and defining what exactly is "un-Thai" here is going to be difficult. The problem seems to be the nipple. After all, most of the rest of Luk-Ket's body is already in the public domain. It appears regularly in the most public places in the kingdom—especially *Thai Rath*'s front page (visited by half the population) and countless magazine covers. We have seen the top of her breasts, the sides, and, only a few days ago, a cheeky glimpse of the bottom part. On a recent magazine cover, only the nipples were obscured by nothing much more than typography. But none of these appearances were deemed threats to the national culture.

Perhaps the problem is that in the fashion show the breast was more dynamic. At work, as it were. But again, other examples have not excited such concern. Recently another starlet appeared on *Thai Rath*'s front page in the process of, ummmm, testing herself for breast cancer. No outcry. Last week on Channel 7's *Saket Khao*, an old village lady was filmed breast-feeding her pet cat. The camera angles were "Thai" so the nipples were always discreetly disguised behind cat fur, but we knew they were there, and certainly at work. But again, no outcry.

But if the problem really is the nipple, what about the case of katoey? As any beach-goer knows, they like to show off their breasts because these represent a significant investment. Technically katoey are still male, and hence the nipple is a male nipple and should not be a problem. But does all the silicone or saline behind the nipple in fact change its legal status?

Is the problem not in fact the nipple but the breast? Drafting this law is going to be tough. Over to the Council of State . . .

Calling this breast's public appearance "un-Thai" suggests it contravenes Thai traditions. Nothing could be further from the truth. The Europeans who arrived in the early nineteenth century found Siamese women left their breasts uncovered as a matter of course. Upper-class women might wear a loose upper cloth but "it forms an imperfect covering for the bosoms which are much more frequently wholly exposed and unprotected." Peasant women often donned a singlet while working for practical reasons, but took it off when the work was over.

The Europeans were horrified by all this exposed flesh, both male and female. One European mistook King Mongkut's brother for a "savage" because of his brief clothing, and was gobsmacked to discover the prince was such a learned and sophisticated man. Under this prudish European gaze, both Siamese men and women began to wear more clothes. By the late nineteenth century, women in Bangkok usually covered their breasts. In the villages the change came much slower. Even today in more remote parts, older women still leave their upper body uncovered as a matter of course.

So the "un-Thai" labeling here has nothing to do with history and tradition, but is totally modern, rather urban, and very Western-influenced. This kind of "culture" is being re-created all the time. The historical dramas which have become so popular in cinema and TV play a part. Take the current TV series, *Sai Lohit* (blood line), set in the final days of the Ayutthaya period. The costuming is splendid, and its exoticness lays a quiet claim to authenticity. The bare torsos of the males, resplendent with tattoos, might be close to historical accuracy. But to render the females authentic would mean cropping their hair short, blackening their teeth, and leaving their breasts exposed. Yet this would be, ummmm, "un-Thai." Also the audiences would not like it and the starlets would revolt. So instead they have luxuriously long hair done up into funny styles in order to appear different from today (and hence "authentic"), while their teeth gleam, and no more flesh is exposed than a single shoulder.

The point is not whether these dramas ought to be authentic. The point is that "culture" is being created and re-created all the time. The Ministry of Culture is not engaged in preserving something. Rather it is creating it, reflecting a modern, urban, middle-class, prudish view of the world.

And maybe a bit more than that. Most societies try to discipline women by imposing codes of behavior. In the past, it was easy to distinguish between good girls, who were conservative and demure, and bad girls who wore too little and did wrong things. But Luk-Ket's publication of her own body is a key part of a wider movement which is wrecking these old codes. She takes most of her clothes off in public again and again, but you cannot mistake her for a bad girl. Rather, she is a symbol of female independence.

After the nipple crisis, she was interviewed on TV. Her story was strikingly familiar. She needs to work to buy her mother a house, and to put her sister through education. She had a chance to have a sugar daddy patron, but she prefers to work, be independent, and have a more egalitarian love-life. Above all, she comes across as someone in command of herself.

Is it a coincidence that this nipple crisis blew up just when the Ministry of Culture changed from female to male hands? If Thai women are allowed to use their own surnames, flash their nipples, and whoever knows whatever next, then it probably won't do much damage to "Thai culture" (whatever that is), but it will chip away further at the old belief that women are the property of men.

BEATING A BEAUTY

27 June 2005

She was raped twice. She was abducted against her will, and kept locked up with chains. She was hit several times, throttled, punched in the stomach, thrown to the floor, and threatened with guns and other weapons. She was tricked into a fruitless jungle trek equipped with a pair of sandals. She appeared week-after-week with bruised face, tearful eyes, or blood trickling from her mouth.

This was not some poor defenseless victim. The character was supposed to be an ultra-modern woman with an overseas PhD. Nobody in the story seemed to live in a house smaller than an airport terminal.

Phloeng Phayu (Firestorm), the prime-time drama serial that ended last week, was an epic on the theme of the abuse of women. The lead actress, Patchara Chaichua (Um) has been voted the country's prettiest and sexiest star. The series was about watching someone this lovely and famous getting beaten up, over and over again.

There was a labyrinthine plot about disputed inheritance and sibling jealousies, but that was just there to spin things out and keep the usual character actors in paid employment. There was also a Fatal Misunderstanding to explain away the bad behavior, but it was a very thin excuse.

There was also a little bit of moral relativism. The really nasty rapist (he drooled like a mad dog) got his come-uppance by shooting himself while trying to rape her again and murder his own daughter at the same time. Instead, it was the not-quite-so-nasty rapist who eventually got the girl.

The two suitors who didn't enjoy beating her around got nowhere. One disqualified himself by being a farang, and the other by being too nice to be true. When she threw him over, he took it out on the sea rather than hitting her around the head. What a wimp.

And what a message.

For viewers who are upset this series has ended, the channel ran two trailers of its successors. In one, a father was beating his daughter around the head. In the other, a woman was throttled, punched, threatened with guns and sharp objects, and then had her throat slit.

This is family entertainment. It runs in prime time. The prime minister told the nation how much he enjoyed it, which is a kind of endorsement.

This epic on the abuse of women was running at the same time as the *Big Brother* reality show which caused controversy. Two of the young people in a group closeted together in a house seemed to fall in love. The self-appointed keepers of national morality objected to scenes of them having a cuddle as "un-Thai."

Firestorm attracted no equivalent complaint. We should not be allowed to see a little cuddle reflecting young love, but multiple rape, abduction, and sundry violence reflecting male domination are fine. The cuddle appeared on a cable channel with few viewers. The multiple abuse was on prime-time free-to-air with a huge audience. The cuddle was apparently spontaneous. The multiple abuse was brought to us through the talents of a large group of writers, directors, actors with the help of a lot of expensive equipment. The cuddle is "un-Thai," but . . .

The display of violence against women in TV dramas is not new but has increased sharply. Other TV shows follow the same trend. Game shows often have one male comedian dressed up as a woman beaten around by the others. An ad showing a woman repeatedly slapping herself for having oily skin is among several that have flirted with violence against women.

What is going on here?

In part this probably reflects a general increase in social violence under the current government. The drug wars, extrajudicial killings, repeated assassination of activists, and unexplained disappearances create a climate in which the public display of violence as entertainment becomes more acceptable.

In part, it may reflect the general dumbing down of the media. The Thaksin government has successfully drained the electronic media of any social and political content. Five years ago, scriptwriters were able to build drama series around real issues including "influence," corruption, Burmese refugees, and even the abuse of political power. Now they are limited to the stale old genres. It is no surprise that family dramas are becoming more labyrinthine, ghost stories more outrageous, and thrillers more violent.

But is there something else which focuses this dramatic violence so much against women?

The social power of women has grown significantly over the past decade. There are more women in parliament than before, and significantly more women at the upper levels of the public service. Some like Khunying Pornthip Rojanasunan and Khunying Jaruvarn Maintaka have bigger public profiles than possibly any predecessors. Women have overtaken men in the enrollment and exam results in universities. A few more high-profile women have appeared in big business. Women rather than men brought the medals back from the last Olympics. The first pop singer going out from Thailand to the world is female (Tata Young).

Of course, the male-female imbalance is still huge. What is important, though, is the trend.

The television media seem to reflect a deep male anxiety about all of this. One of the persistent themes of TV dramas in recent years is about women who come to a sticky end by being too ambitious in business, love, or the gangster world.

Chang Noi would like to propose a new reality TV show. A group of TV producers, directors, scriptwriters, and channel executives is closeted in a house. An SMS vote is held to select a two-hour segment of prime-time viewing. Each participant is then subject to the same acts of violence against women which are portrayed on screen. On the evidence of the final episode of *Firestorm*, complete with its prelude and trailers, they would each suffer being raped, manacled in chains, thrown to the ground, threatened with guns and sharp objects, hit around the head several times, punched in the stomach, throttled, and having their throats slit.

Of course, nobody would win.

Tooth and claw

NGOS, VIOLENCE, AND MONEY

3 January 2003

On radio on 21 December, Thaksin identified a specific group of "NGO workers who use violence." These people in fact "live well but like making trouble." He later referred to them as "anarchists."[39] Chavalit Yongchaiyudh added they are bent on "overthrowing capitalism." Thaksin earlier said NGOs are financed by foreign organizations "which do not want Thailand to develop." They stir up trouble, record it on video, and send the tapes to their foreign sponsors to secure more funding. Now we know. Thailand is threatened by a foreign-financed conspiracy of rich anarchists.

Who are the NGOs? It's true that most of the first generation of Thailand's NGO workers came from the comfortably-off middle class. They were caught up in the student radicalism of the 1970s, and later transferred their idealism to grassroots work. Many of the public faces of the NGO movement still come from this group. But lower down the ranks, the social complexion is changing.

Lamphaen comes from a Lue village in Nan. Her family, unlike their neighbors, kept up the Lue tradition of hand-weaving. This generated just enough extra income to keep her in school. Lamphaen became the first person from her village to get a university degree. She rejected the secure job in government or the lucrative one in business. Instead she joined an NGO. She found a few simple ways to make weaving more

---

39. On 20 December 2002, a hundred demonstrators and sixteen police were injured after violence erupted in a demonstration against the Thai-Malaysia gas pipeline outside a hotel in Hat Yai where Thaksin was meeting with Mahathir. Immediately after, Thaksin railed threateningly against "violent" NGOs. A few days later, a tape of the incident was shown in Thammasat University. The tape mostly came from one camera with no editing (the clock was visible). It clearly showed the demonstrators, passive and praying, being attacked by the police.

efficient and profitable. She organized neighboring families into groups. She found new channels to market the products. Now many villages in the area produce lots of cloth. And a lot more kids stay in school.

Lamphaen's example is multiplied many times. Few NGO recruits over the past decade come from the urban middle class. Student radicalism and idealism declined, while the commercial job market expanded. Most new recruits come from the villages and the urban underclass. Often they have profited from the expansion of education, but not used this as a means of personal escape. Instead they have joined NGOs as a way to develop the society from which they come. This is especially true of new NGO workers in resource and environment issues. Quietly and invisibly, NGO politics are becoming class politics.

What do the NGOs do? Some months ago, Chang Noi had the privilege to attend the strategy review meeting of a big national NGO network. No plush hotel. No travel expenses. No fancy cakes at tea breaks. Not even any furniture. The meeting was held in an unoccupied house loaned by a friend. For the two days of plenary sessions, delegates sat on the bare concrete floor. The breakouts were under a tree in the garden. Accommodation was on mats upstairs. Catering was provided by some pushcart vendors from up the road.

Of course several NGO workers are supported by foreign funds. But it's pretty meager.

The purpose of the meeting was to review the network's strategy in the light of past experience. Many participants noted the situation is changing very rapidly. Earlier, NGO workers had played an important role in organizing local people, providing them with information, and helping them express grievances to bureaucrats and politicians. But local groups have developed very quickly. They have learned how to get good information and technical help. They have absorbed the techniques of organization, petition, and protest. They have set up their own networks. The role of the NGO workers has moved from foreground to background.

What are the NGOs up against? Non-violence has been one of the guiding faiths of the Thai NGO movement. The 1970s generation reacted strongly against the violence of left-right confrontation. But non-violence is a very delicate practice. Demonstrations always have an element of provocation. And the Thai authorities have a history of using violence.

The videotape of the Hat Yai clash on 20 December is very explicit. As the police move forward to clear the demo, the speaker on the top of the sound truck calls to the demonstrators to stay calm. Sit down. Don't react. Let them beat us if they want to. Don't be provoked. Beware the third hand. A policeman tries to climb onto the truck and smash the sound system with a stick. There is no trouble yet. Apparently he wants to silence this appeal to non-violence. It's not clear what right he has to destroy property. Unfortunately, he slips and falls back three times. This little tragi-comedy lasts several minutes. No superior intervenes to stop his very visible effort, so presumably he is acting in line with orders. Eventually he gets so frustrated he beats his stick on the windscreen. And then he hits the driver.

As a former government security expert commented after seeing this tape, the Hat Yai clash happened because the authorities treat demonstrators as enemies.

The NGO movement has become so prominent in Thailand because of the failure of bureaucrats to deliver services and the failure of politicians to represent the people. As Kasian Tejapira remarked last week, NGOs are a service which Thailand's middle class gets for free (but fails to appreciate).

The movement is big, varied, and far from perfect. But it is not a foreign-funded plot riddled with anarchists. The movement's little secret is that it depends on a rather small number of people working very hard with very limited resources. It's strength comes from the issues themselves, and from the base of popular support. It's also changing. Its center of gravity is moving into the localities, and into the hands of a new generation of more local activists.

Thaksin wants to help "the poor" because their complaints are bad for business. But he doesn't understand the intensity and proliferation of local discontent. He wants to turn middle-class opinion against NGOs by demonizing an imagined anarchist, violent, foreign-funded minority. At the same time he said "I am ready to provide funding for the 96 percent majority of NGOs." He thinks he can buy NGOs as easily as MPs.

ANYTHING UNDER A DICTATOR'S SUN

20 January 2003

To encourage the police to rid Thailand of drugs within three months, the prime minister quoted the 1950s police chief, Phao Siyanon: "there is nothing under the sun that the Thai police cannot do."

The achievements for which Phao and his police force have gone down in history are assassinating MPs and smuggling drugs.

Phao was an army officer who married the daughter of a powerful general, Phin Choonhavan. He took part in the November 1947 coup which ended one of the repeated attempts to found democracy in Thailand. He was made deputy director of the police but soon had higher ambitions. He demanded that the interior minister promote him to the director job. The minister refused. Phao challenged him to a duel.

He got the job anyway in 1951. By that time the CIA had identified Phao as their contact for carrying out covert operations both in Thailand and neighboring countries. They gave Phao's police lots of hardware—guns, speedboats, planes, tanks, helicopters—and lots of training. The police became an alternative army and has never lost that militarized character.

Phao used these resources not only for the CIA's secret operations, but for terrorizing political opponents. He developed a circle of *asawin waen phet*, knights of the diamond ring, for these special operations.

In March 1949, the MPs for Roi Et, Maha Sarakham, Ubon, and one associate, all of whom had previously served as cabinet ministers, were arrested on hazy charges of plotting a rebellion. While being transported from one jail to another under police escort, they were shot dead. Phao explained that the police detail had been attacked by a gang of robbers. Nobody believed him. Many years later, after Phao's fall, the real culprits were tried. A witness described how Phao had held a party after the event and distributed 30,000 baht each to around thirty police.

In December 1952, Tiang Sirikhan disappeared. He was MP for Sakon Nakhon and one of the bravest opponents of military dictatorship. Phao announced Tiang had been spotted fleeing to Burma. Doctored photos were produced showing him with Ho Chi Minh. Before long, four bodies were found in a charcoal pit in Kanchanaburi. They had been strangled and burnt, but were easily identifiable as Tiang and three associates.

Ari Liwara, the most successful newspaper publisher of the time, was pressured to sell his businesses to Phao. He refused. In March 1953 he was shot dead on his honeymoon in Hua Hin.

Phon Malithong, the MP for Samut Sakhon, exposed Phao's activities in parliament on several occasions. In March 1954, Phon and a police informer were strangled and dumped in the Chaophraya River tied to concrete posts. Phon's car was dismantled and thrown in the river, too.

There were many other deaths including army officers, Thai-Muslim leaders, and even possibly a Laotian minister. When an American ambassador was killed in a truck crash in Hua Hin, the reaction was revealing. Even Phao's CIA patrons jumped to the conclusion that it might be Phao's handiwork, until the evidence showed otherwise.

Phao also became enormously rich. Partly this was by taking control of government monopolies, and blackmailing companies to give him shareholdings and put him on the board. But a substantial contribution came from the opium trade.

At that time, opium was still sold legally in Thailand under a government monopoly. But the big profits were in export. The Golden Triangle was just developing into the world's major area of production. Phao's police was the perfect organization to move the goods from the Triangle into the world market. Police escorts met the convoys at the Burmese border and took them to Chiang Mai or Lampang. From there the goods traveled to Bangkok by train or plane. The maritime police then guarded their transfer to freighters in the gulf.

Surachart Bamrungsuk concluded that Phao's police by 1955 was "the largest opium-trafficking syndicate in Thailand involved in every phase of the narcotics trade."

This did not always go smoothly. The army was equally well equipped to provide this escort service, and the two tended to compete. On one occasion in 1950, the army was escorting a convoy to Lampang when the police set an ambush and demanded the goods. The two sides dug in for a firefight and faced off for two days. Phao and the army chief had to turn up in person to negotiate an armistice. A director of the metropolitan police, who also tried to interfere with Phao's shipments, was shot dead "while resisting arrest."

Phao's police conducted pantomime seizures of drugs to give an image of drug suppression. Sometimes these dramas went over the top. In 1955, the police made a record capture of 20 tons of opium, and Phao himself collected a massive reward on behalf of an informer. When asked to display the haul, Phao said it had been thrown in the sea. The public disbelief almost undid him. On another occasion, a seized cache of high-grade opium turned out to be low-grade mud.

In 1957, Phao lost power and fled to Switzerland. A couple of his "knights" went with him. A newspaperman went to visit. Phao was living in high style, even with an English chauffeur. In interview, he confessed to most of the political killings. He explained that he had "wanted to be a big man," and that he had been acting on orders of his boss (Phibun). The newspaperman subtitled his book of these confessions, "The iron man of Asia." A *New York Times* writer preferred "a superlative crook." A senior Thai diplomat of the time called him "the worst man in the whole history of modern Thailand."

Under a dictatorship, and with the right mentality, there is indeed "nothing under the sun that the Thai police cannot do." Drugs are bad. So too are the abuse of power and the sacrifice of human rights.

Phao's famous saying on the Thai police has a second line that is less often remembered. In full it reads, "there is nothing under the sun that the Thai police cannot do, in ways that do not conflict with morality, custom, fine traditions, and the law of the land."[40]

---

40. This quote was formerly emblazoned on the police website, but it has since disappeared.

MASS MURDER IN THE MILK BAR

18 February 2003

They sat down in a trendy new eating place in the department store. A couple of young professionals. One of them looked very gloomy.

Jit: It must be around two hundred bodies now.[41] It's mass murder. If the government is behind it, then it would be hard to find anything similar in the world outside a revolution or a civil war.

Jai: But what makes you think it's the government? The prime minister denies it.

Jit: Well, for a start because the interior minister announced it. He said something like, we're going to kill them and seize their property so their children do not benefit. Of course, other government ministers came out and gave totally contradictory statements. But that's normal. A minister did announce this.

Jai: So you don't believe it's other drug dealers who are doing these killings?

Jit: Don't you think it's a bit strange that so many of these killings are the same? If this was a panic reaction among drug dealers, you would have expected things to be a bit more varied. And messier. Some knife fights. The odd grenade. Explosives. Whatever. But no. Most seem to be highly efficient executions by hand arms. Very professional.

Jai: Maybe. But who cares? These are bad people. They don't care who gets hurt by the drugs they sell. They have been warned many times. I agree with Thaksin. We shouldn't have any sympathy. We should care more about the risk to the police.

---

41. Thaksin's "war on drugs" was launched on 1 February 2003. In the next seven weeks, government PR claimed around 2,700 "drug dealers" were killed. In 2007, an investigation headed by the former attorney-general, Kanit na Nakhon concluded that at least 1,400 of those killed had no connection to drug trading (*Nation*, 27 November 2007).

Jit: I just think the authorities have to act within the law. If they don't, why should anybody else. Look at the destruction of the bars in Sukumwit Soi 10, or even the riot in Phnom Penh. Someone decides there's a bigger reason which justifies them to defy the law. That can be getting your property back or salvaging the honor of the nation. Anything.

Jai: But there is a difference in this case. Lots of people support this campaign against the drug dealers. They're fed up with the fact that the dealers have got away with this for so long. They like Thaksin for being decisive.

Jit: You're probably right. But does that mean the government can now do anything as long as it feels it has some kind of vague popular support? There are consequences, you know. Despite being a Buddhist country, there's a very violent streak in the culture. Not so long ago, when law enforcement was very weak, people were used to settling their own problems using violence. Then when we were fighting communism, people in uniform got used to doing terrible things in the name of saving the country. Eventually that results in events like the October 1976 and May 1992 massacres. There are not many countries where a university has been subjected to armed assault, and a street demo has been cleared using the methods of jungle warfare. Look at elections even now. How many canvassers get shot every time? This anti-drug campaign promotes this sort of thing.

Jai: So you worry it encourages other people.

Jit: Yes. Suppose I decide this is a great chance to take revenge on my business rival. I hire a hit man. Get some pills planted on the body. The police who find these pills are happy because they get a bounty. The provincial governor breathes a sigh of relief because he has another statistic. And these cases never go anywhere because the police cannot decide whether the dead man was killed because of his four minor wives, his five shady businesses, or his role as an election agent.

There has been a strong force in support of non-violence over recent years. But events like this push things the other way. Just look at last week. A *Thai Rath* reporter assassinated in Phuket. A grenade launched at a big political family in Khorat. A vendor shot on a Bangkok street. Is this the open season? Should we be surprised?

Jai: But we know those events are different. It's very clear. They are about business conflict, or political conflict, or something else.

Jit: In these cases, yes. But there are going to be other cases which are not so clear. I'd feel safer if I thought we had a good chance of getting the information to make the distinction. But it has become difficult to trust the media these days. Especially TV. The news reports are like government propaganda. The current affairs programs have become little more than "Meet the Minister." Even the dramas on the army-owned channels are thinly disguised PR for the military. It's like we've gone back before 1992, before 1988, maybe even earlier. This combination of media control and violence is horribly familiar. Suppose the local branch of some political party decides to get a step ahead in the next election by picking off a few of the rival canvassers.

Jai: Okay. But suppose it works. Suppose we do get rid of drugs. Suppose a few hundred real drug dealers die and maybe a handful of others are killed on the side. Wouldn't that be worth it? Wouldn't it be an acceptable cost?

Jit: But how do you make the calculation? Would ten innocent deaths be ok? How about a hundred? Or a thousand? Besides, what makes you think that the success would stick? The authorities have been after the *ya ba* dealers for six to seven years. We have had national campaign after national campaign. Signs everywhere saying selling drugs is like selling the country. Pa Prem making appeals on TV. Ads showing officials being locked in jail. Pop stars making soulful appeals. Marches, concerts. But none of it works. Not law enforcement, peer pressure, appeals to nationalism, nothing. Only mass murder. What does that tell us? The problem goes deep. This may be a quick solution, but it may not solve the real problem and so it won't last. What happens then? We do it again?

Jai: Drink your milk.

POLARIZED OPINIONS OVER THE DRUG WAR

8 December 2003

The end of the government's campaign against methamphetamines has polarized opinions. On one side, the government has declared victory in a blizzard of statistics. Prices are up, volume down, and a handful of key dealers are in jail. On the other side, human rights advocates say there is only one important statistic—the 2,626 people murdered. Whether the police did it, or opened the door for others, or simply let the murderers get away with it, makes no difference. This is not the rule of law but the law of the jungle.

Behind this polarization, there is a very difficult question: why has this Buddhist society overwhelmingly approved this killing? Last March, 72 percent of people told the Rangsit Poll they approved of the campaign. At that time, the nightly TV news carried clip after clip of bodies lying in pools of blood. A few days earlier, a nine-year-old boy had been shot dead in the crossfire. Despite this, 76 percent of the poll respondents thought government should continue the violent methods of preemptive and extrajudicial killing.

Another poll found that 70 percent of monks supported the campaign. And in a Ramkhamhaeng poll, almost two-thirds said, specifically, that human rights advocates should stop calling for justice for drug suspects.

There is no doubt the campaign was popular. There is also no doubt that many petty users and traders who deserved at most a mild punishment (and several totally innocent people) were unjustly served with the death penalty. Jaran Cosananund, a Ramkhamhaeng law lecturer and human rights supporter, has wrestled with the question why Thai society has embraced this obvious violence and cruelty.[42]

---

42. Jaran Cosanund's article on "Human rights and the war on drugs" appeared in *Thailand Human Rights Journal*, I, 2003.

One explanation is that Thai society values a kind of crude pragmatism more than any systematic ethics. If something works, then it's okay. This is based in turn on a crude egoism. People look after themselves and have little empathy for the rights and dignity of others. Probably this is part of the heavy legacy of absolutism and dictatorship in the society's history. The whole idea of rights, human dignity, and the rule of law has never meant all that much. The result today is "a political culture of self-interest, looking after oneself, and the devil take the hindmost." The government can exploit this mentality to argue that the end justifies the means. Normal judicial process can be bypassed because conquering drugs is a "national" goal.

But this explanation may focus too narrowly on a supposed failing of "Thai" society and ethics. If you look around the world, there is a trend to "populist justice." Under globalization, the world is becoming more socially divided, more riven by conflicts, and more violent. Terrorism is on the rise at the international level, and violent crime is in everyone's backyard. Formal processes (police, law, courts) cannot deal with it, so other methods are sought. The US, the cradle of human rights, began to destroy its own citizens' rights when it got desperate in its own drug wars. And now it does the same at the international level in the campaign against "terrorism."

It is often the poor who suffer most from violent crime and support this "populist justice." When *ya ba* boomed in Thailand, a lot of ordinary people became victims of the trade. In effect, their rights were being violated. Some lost their rights to livelihood or education. Families lost their rights to peace and contentment. But advocates of human rights paid no attention to this. Instead they focused on the violations of the human rights of those targeted on the government's blacklists. Perhaps, Jaran gently suggests, this was a bit one-eyed. Perhaps it was not surprising that the mass of people thought human rights idealists had got their priorities wrong.

Maybe the problem is broader. Maybe most people don't care about human rights at all because these rights have no meaning for themselves. Ordinary people in Thai society, especially the poor, have low expectations of the police and judicial system. They expect them to be corrupt and biased against them. They are used to having their own rights violated. They face violence in their everyday lives as a matter of course. What difference, then, are they likely to see between a proper judicial punishment on the one hand, and an extra-judicial killing on the other? Where is the magic in such ideas as human rights, human dignity, and the rule of law if there are no rational reasons for ordinary people to value them? In Jaran's words, "It is hardly surprising that people who face crime problems should be prepared to sacrifice or ignore human rights principles, and reject the value of human rights in general, on grounds they lack any real significance and are too much of a luxury for their society."

This comes down to a chicken-and-egg problem. People will only value human rights and the rule of law if these concepts have real benefits for themselves. But this can never happen as long as government takes advantage of people's crude pragmatism and low expectations of the judicial system to bypass rights and the rule of law at every opportunity.

What bothers Jaran most is the polarization of views because it blocks any dialogue to break this circular logic. As a start, everyone involved needs to recognize their own ignorance and limitations. Those planning and enforcing the drug policy may be just as confused ethically as someone high on *ya ba*. Those protesting violation of human rights by the police may be shutting their eyes to much larger violations committed by the drug traders. The only way to break down this polarization is compassion on both sides.

SHOOTING THE MESSENGER

26 April 2004

The skirmishes between the Thai government and human rights organizations are escalating towards a full-blown war. This is silly, and too many people are getting hurt.

Hina Jilani's job at the UN is to monitor the safety and freedom of people around the world who work on behalf of human rights. She compiles an annual report about them worldwide, and makes occasional special reports on individual countries.

She came to Thailand for eight days in May 2003, in the aftermath of the first, bloody phase of the government's war on drugs. She has now presented her report.

She thanks government for making her visit possible. She notes she had very free access. She praises ways in which this government has targeted poverty. But there the diplomatic politeness runs out.

Thailand used to be a beacon for human rights work in the region. Its own importance was magnified because the situation in neighboring countries was so much worse. For the Burmese in particular, Thailand's freedoms were vital as an example. Hence the fact that Thailand is "no longer as comfortable a location for human rights defenders and their organizations" is doubly unfortunate.

She is concerned that the current government has declared war on the NGO movement. In the past, the vitality of Thailand's NGOs contributed a lot to Thailand's good image in the world. But now the government tries to undermine their legitimacy by denigrating them publicly. It tries to block any funding from abroad. It applies harassment through rules and regulations. She concludes, "Some officials perceive the function of serving the people as exclusive to the Government." They think NGOs just get in the way.

As Jilani summarizes, "There is limited acceptance among some authorities of the concept of peaceful dissent." This is bad itself. It also sends a clear message to people with bad intentions. The result is evident from the cases listed in Jilani's report.

Boonyong Intawong, a community leader protesting against the health and environmental impact of a rock quarry in Chiang Rai, was killed in December 2002. Boonsom Nimnoi, a community leader opposing a Phetchaburi plantation, was killed in September 2002. Suwat Wongpiasathit, an activist protesting a landfill in Samut Prakan, was shot dead in March 2001, a day before he was due to speak to a Senate committee on the environment.

Jurin Rachaphol, a Phuket campaigner against the destruction of mangrove swamps, was killed in January 2002. Pitak Tonewuth, a Ramkhamhaeng University environmental activist, was killed in May 2001. Sompol Chanapol, another leader of a local conservation group, was killed in July 2001. Luechai Yarangsi, president of an environmental group in Lampang, was shot but survived.

Preecha Thongphan, a community leader opposing a water treatment project in Nakhon Si Thammarat, was killed in September 2002. Jintana Kaewkao, opponent of the power projects in Prachuap, was shot in her home in January 2002. Her colleague, Yuthana Khaemakriangkrai, was shot on the following day.

This litany of cases is so striking because the pattern is the same: an activist opposing some attempt to wreck the local environment is killed. These incidents come from all over the country. This handful of cases includes just those which Jilani managed to document during a short eight-day visit.

Jilani was told that police made some arrests in some of these cases, but did not bring one single suspect to trial. She draws the quiet conclusion that this must be because of "collusion between local authorities and commercially powerful actors from the private sector." Translated from reportspeak: big people shoot little people who get in their way.

Another very vulnerable group includes leaders or supporters of hill communities. Jilani steers clear of the drug war, claiming that extrajudicial killings are not part of her work. But she does note that hill community leaders who had been critical of police work in the past tended to find their way onto the blacklists of drug suspects. A group of community forest activists who set up roadblocks to exclude loggers from a forest were attacked and shot at by an armed band. A leader of the Northern Peasants Federation was shot and injured in Lamphun.

Sadly, the government has reacted to this report rather negatively. It has tried to suggest that the report was prematurely leaked (versions have been officially available on Internet for some time). The foreign minister has made some huffy comments. The Thai representative to the UN responded to the report by rebuking Jilani as an ungrateful guest, and accusing her of not knowing how to write a report. He says: "we obviously cannot accept generalized comments and the inclusion of unsubstantiated information." He complains that Jilani's visit has not turned out to be a "learning experience," implying that is her fault.

Whisper "human rights" now, and the government goes into full counter-strike mode. This is sad. The root problem is obviously the drug war. Jilani skips past this but does note "the intense sensitivity of the Government on this issue." By refusing to engage in any sensible discussion of what happened during the drug war, the government digs itself deeper and deeper into a hole. The more antagonistic the government becomes to human rights and their defenders, the more it encourages those who regularly violate human rights for fun, power, or profit.

The fact that the ministerial team at the forefront of the drug war (Chavalit, Thammarak) has been pulled off the case in the south is very significant. Thaksin knows what forces are at work. The costs of allowing them free rein in the south have become too high. But breaking down the broader antagonism between this government and the human rights community will be much more difficult. This government has identified itself too deeply with some of the bad old authoritarian ways. And that means people at the grassroots will continue to get shot for defending the environment, their communities, and their way of life.

DARKNESS AND LIGHT

13 September 2004

The court action which Shin Corp has launched against the NGO activist Supinya Klangnarong for alleged defamation is not the only such legal action under way. There are at least three. In the other two cases, one is still under preparation, and the other is keeping a low profile. The common factor is that each of these legal actions is launched by a company in the Shin Group (by three different ones). It is doubtful that this is a matter of pure coincidence.

Such legal action can be a very effective form of intimidation. The scales are so unevenly balanced. The 400 million baht sum claimed in damages is, on the one hand, equivalent to 2,777 years of Supinya's modest salary, and on the other, roughly equal to the revenue of Shin Corp over one week. For the corporation, the case is something for their legal department to take care of. But for Supinya or any similar defendant, it is both practical hassle and mental strain. Supinya admits that, despite putting on a brave and bright face, she is feeling pretty bad.

As many people have noted, the statements about Shin Corp which have got her into trouble do not seem especially strong or especially different from what many other people have said, both before and since. Probably that is because these are not the sole or main reason why Supinya has been targeted.

What makes her different is that she has been the most high-profile and most effective public advocate for media freedom over the last few years. Targeting her (rather than other critics) has a bigger meaning than defending corporate honor.

Supinya has come out repeatedly to ask the big questions. How come this country, which claims to be marching rapidly towards the first world, has most of its electronic media owned and run by agencies of the state? Twenty years after the collapse of the communist insurgency and fifteen years after the end of the Cold War, why does the army still own two television stations and hundreds of radio stations? Where do their profits go? How come the demand for reform and liberalization of the media, which was so strong after the army shot demonstrators on Bangkok streets in May 1992, has been so well contained? How come ITV, the love-child of the 1992 events, was able to rip up its charter in full public view with total impunity? How come, seven years after passage of the 1997 Constitution, its provisions for transferring control of the electronic media from the state to the people are still not implemented—to the point most people no longer have faith that they will make much difference anyway?

In short, how come the Thailand which wants to be part of the first world, member of OECD, leader of Asia, kitchen of the world, fashion capital, and tourism hub has the electronic media of a banana republic?

Part of Supinya's effectiveness is a matter of pure image. She is campaigning for freedom and openness in media and she does it in a beautifully free and open way. She is the medium and the message. The usual attempts to discredit such critics by alleging that they have ulterior motives simply do not work because the allegations do not seem credible. When she stands up against the former army chief (a man who excused the strange financial dealings in the army TV station as merely an attempt to safeguard the financial interests of the army by subverting the 1997 Constitution), it is light against darkness.

Moreover, the issue of media freedom has become more complex and important in Thailand over the last few years for two reasons.

First, the media and entertainment industries have grown much more lucrative. At Thailand's current stage of development, consumer spending on these items is increasing much faster than the economy as a whole. Companies like Grammy have come from nowhere to rank among the country's largest in just a handful of years. The Maleenont family, holders of the Channel 3 concession, has soared into the top ranks of the wealthy. Media and entertainment are now very big business indeed.

Second, the new populist streak in Thai politics has increased the importance of media image and media exposure. Only a few years ago, the important business of Thai politics was transacted out of sight, in smoky back rooms. That is no longer the case. The 2001 election was a landmark in public campaigning. The desperate smothering of Bangkok in posters over the recent mayoral election (in pursuit of a job which is a joke) shows how much politicians feel they now need public exposure. The electronic media, especially TV, are now vital for gaining and keeping political power.

Those in power understand this very well. Last week, the TV presenter who interviewed Ekkayuth Anchanbutr[43] live had lost his job before the interview was over.

Supinya is probably targeted not just for what she specifically said but more generally for what she stands for. Demands for media freedom are threats to financial interests and political interests. The case against Supinya not only intimidates her specifically, but serves as a more general threat to everybody.

In his speech to the International Conference of Asian Political Parties on 3 September, Thaksin said: "Governments given a mandate to serve the people often end up using such authority to serve their own interests. Governments given the opportunity to enact laws to empower the electorate, often abuse such laws to sustain their own power. And governments chosen to do what is best for the country, often drift towards doing what is best for themselves. I am proud to say that my administration is under no such misconception."

Shine on, Supinya.[44]

---

43. Ekkayuth fled Thailand in 1984 after the collapse of a pyramid investment fraud. In 2004, he enjoyed fleeting fame by criticizing Thaksin.

44. In an interview with *Thai Post* in 2004, Supinya said that Shin Corporation had profited from government actions. The corporation sued both her and the newspaper. On 15 March 2006, Supinya and *Thai Post* were acquitted.

EXPLAINING THAILAND TO THE WORLD

28 March 2005

Thailand's new foreign minister says his priority is to "explain" to the international community about incidents like Krue Se and Tak Bai, and thus overcome the country's bad image on human rights.

Around New Year, Chang Noi watched one of the video CDs of the Tak Bai incident.[45] The showing took place outside Thailand, with an audience of teachers and students mostly from Asian countries ranging from India to Japan. This video compilation began inside the Tak Bai police station at the point when the security forces believed they were coming under fire. It had long sequences showing the arrested demonstrators being tied up, dragged along the ground, kicked and beaten, made to crawl, struggling to avoid drowning in the river, and being thrown on trucks. It ended with a group of senators visiting a detention center. The footage clearly came from several different cameramen, and had been spliced together without much editing. The picture quality was often poor, but the overall story was very clear.

At the end of the one-hour showing, there was first a stunned silence, and then a lively discussion. Thai and non-Thai, Muslim and non-Muslim, all had something to say.

One historian who studies Malaysia told the group that this incident was very similar to others in the past. He knew of documents going back to the 1840s when Siam faced one of the many revolts provoked by its attempt to control the Malay states in the mid peninsula. People had been arrested, maltreated, and died in custody in large numbers. Such

---

45. On 25 October 2004 in Tak Bai, Narathiwat Province, a demonstration demanded the release of six arrested men. Hundreds of the demonstrators were rounded up and transported by truck to a detention camp. On arrival, seventy-eight had died, principally from suffocation as they had been lying stacked in five or six horizontal layers. Another seven died from being shot.

incidents happened again around 1900, and perhaps later also. He asked whether the Thai state had any long-run policy to treat people from this area in this way. If not, why did such incidents seem to recur?

Another Asian member of the audience asked about the treatment of those arrested. Being forced to crawl along the ground with hands tied behind the back, or being put in the river and having to struggle to avoid drowning, probably qualified as torture. This obviously did not happen casually but was very organized and must have been ordered by somebody. Who gave the orders? How high up? Would anyone be held responsible?

One of the few non-Asians in the audience then made a comment. He had expected to see pictures of the security forces trying to disperse a demonstration. Instead the operation was much more like an attack or a military charge. The demonstrators were completely surrounded. They could not "disperse" because there was no way for them to run away. Were the security personnel intent on capturing as many of the demonstrators as possible? Are demonstrators presumed to be criminals?

This prompted comment from an Asian political scientist who has studied security forces throughout the region. He was simply dumbfounded at the crude tactics of the security forces. They did not seem to have any riot control equipment. They were all carrying weapons with live ammunition—with the inevitable results.

In countries like the Philippines and Indonesia, where the security forces often had to deal with insurgents or demonstrators in remote areas, they had equipped themselves appropriately, and learned tactics of riot control which did not provoke violence. In places like Korea, where there were often demonstrations by students and workers in city locations, again the security forces had studied how to deal with them appropriately. There was a lot of learning available, particularly from the British army which had a long history of combating the troubles in Northern Ireland.

The political scientist noted that the clumsiness of the security operation reminded him of what happened on the Bangkok streets during May 1992. He asked why the Thai security forces seemed to treat political demonstrators like a wartime enemy. A member of the audience who had inside knowledge replied that the police and soldiers seen in the video seemed to be following standard Thai procedures. If so, the political scientist asked, why did the Thai security forces retain such procedures and not learn from elsewhere?

Discussion then turned to the video's final sequence showing scenes at the detention center a couple of days after the incident. Around a hundred detainees were sitting on the floor in rows and being instructed by a security officer. What was going on? Thai members of the audience had to explain. The instructor was organizing them to sing a kindergarten song about elephants. "Elephant, elephant, elephant; have you ever seen an elephant?" There was another stunned silence. An East Asian member of the audience then began to think aloud. So first we saw the security forces treating people like animals, then treating those who were lucky enough to survive like infants. Do the Thai security forces think that people in their country's far south are infants and animals? If so, does that explain why the situation has become so bad?

The final comment came from someone from one of Thailand's neighboring countries. She understood that the southern problem is complex. The violence perpetrated by the rebels is awful and unacceptable. But the state and its security forces have a special responsibility. Because they claim a monopoly on the legitimate use of violence, they must use that violence within the bounds of certain rules. Given the growth of tensions on a regional and worldwide scale, incidents like Tak Bai have consequences which are not confined within one country's borders. As a neighbor of Thailand, she could not accept the government's argument that Tak Bai was a "domestic" affair and others should not interfere. What, she asked, can all of us do to prevent such incidents happening because their consequences are widespread and far-reaching?

When Thailand's new foreign minister starts "explaining" Tak Bai and other incidents to the international community, he has to answer the sort of questions raised by this audience. But maybe he has started off with the wrong verb. "Explaining" is not what is needed.

NO NEWS IS BAD, BAD NEWS

25 July 2005

Sex, religion, magic, blackmail, lots of money, and lurid visuals. The tale of Nain Ae[46] is the perfect news story of the Thaksin era.

He used to be in the monkhood. He claims to have supernatural powers. His whole body, except the center of his face, is etched with intricate tattoos. Women believe his magic will help them hold onto their men. Thousands have used his services, offering lots of money and their own bodies in return. He kept Viagra under his ritual throne, and secretly videotaped his sessions, perhaps for blackmail. He advertised his services in magazines and on a TV chat show interview. His 5-rai compound has several houses, a boxing ring, and a cockfight pit. He rode around in a Benz. Neighbors told stories of women throwing bags of money over the wall.

This is "value creation" at least as impressive as Thaksin's claim that he can turn "paper into money." More importantly, Nain Ae is just the latest in the string of circus acts that have marked the Thaksin era. Remember the senator and the Japanese gold in a Kanchanaburi cave?[47]

---

46. Harn Raksajit (Nain Ae) persuaded his clients that his magic, fortified through sex with Harn himself, would make them more attractive. His clients included prostitutes and women abandoned by a spouse. When the police raided his Saraburi house, Harn was in bed with a nineteen-year-old bar girl. The raid was instigated after Harn's wife lodged a complaint. In December 2006, Harn was sentenced to a hundred years in jail, and required to return 910,000 baht to thirty-three women he had defrauded.

47. In early 2001, Chaowarin Latthasaksiri, senator for Ratchaburi, announced that he could locate the treasure which the Japanese army had abandoned in Lijia Cave in Kanchanaburi at the end of the Second World War. The US$25 billion in gold and US$55 billion in US bonds would save the country from the financial crisis by paying off the national debt. Thaksin blessed the search, personally visited the site, and offered to use his position as prime minister to get satellite sensing information from the US. When Chaowarin produced as evidence a bond certificate dated 1934, exactly like those that had recently surfaced in a scam in the Philippines, the project collapsed.

Remember Chuwit and his promise to expose the whole police hierarchy? Remember the Miss Universe extravaganza? Remember APEC?

Nain Ae might be worth a couple of inches in those newspaper sidebars offering a little light relief to the serious business of reading the news. But the Nain Ae circus has made repeated performances on press and TV for several weeks.

The popular daily, *Thai Rath*, and its imitators have long been famous for their front pages palpitating with violent and lurid stories. A sub-segment of the magazine market offers readers a concentrated installment of curiosity and gore every fortnight. But over the last four years, this genre has escaped from these well-known locations, and spread widely in the more "serious" press and the electronic media.

Newspapers are self-censoring so much potential news and opinion that there are acres of space to be filled with something else. The nation's newspapers may now have more international news than anywhere else in the world. The space devoted to celebrity trivia has roughly doubled. But the real boom has been in "human interest" stories.

Often these are rather ordinary stories which editors decide are worth an extraordinary amount of room. A drunk woman who trashes a phone booth at 2 a.m. makes the news page. A student who dies falling under a bus merits ten column-inches of text. A blind vendor who falls down a drain gets a color picture. A baby dying in a nursery makes the front page. A strip show in an army camp is a story which extends over several days with investigative reporters fearlessly interviewing army brass for their reactions.

But very often these stories qualify for newsworthiness on one of two counts. Either they portray a truly inhuman character. Or they have an element of bizarre irrationality.

A man is not content with abducting a twelve-year-old and keeping her as his sex slave, but sends her out to work to keep him as well. Teenage thieves axe a man to death, accidentally chopping off a kid's ear in the process, then take the kid to hospital before spending the stolen money (one thousand baht) on computer games and gambling. An insurance salesman kills himself by sealing his nose and mouth with superglue. A man stressed out by the rape of his sister kills his own father, brother, and another sister with a machete. A three-year-old is beaten to death by her stepfather. A pig farmer has her brain eaten away by maggots which got up her nose. The police decide a man found riddled with five fatal bullet wounds was a suicide. A father whips his daughter with a coat-hanger for getting her multiplication tables wrong. A noodle vendor presses charges against a fourteen-year-old boy for wasting chili powder. A policeman shoots a traffic offender and then himself. Lottery vendors steal a winning ticket back from a customer then bargain over sharing out the prize. (All these stories appeared in the last couple of months.)

Often the authorities are very willing accessories to this project to fill up the news space. A serial killer of sex workers is taken on a national tour to reenact his crimes with a flock of reporters in tow.

In the pre-Thaksin era, the general impression from the stories in the nation's press was of a society becoming more organized, more assertive, more together. Local organizations were mushrooming. People were demanding their rights. NGOs were knitting together networks which spanned region and nation. People outside the usual chattering classes were engaging in debates on reform.

The general impression from the press today is of a society falling apart, full of violence and bizarre irrationality.

Television is similar. The pathetic list of government PR announcements that has come to replace the news is so short and boring that TV channels also add human interest stories. Most channels now have a regular slot highlighting the plight of the less fortunate in society. A typical story shows some individual rendered helpless, perhaps just by old age and poverty, but often by some physical disability too. This person is shown living alone, or accompanied by a child or some shattered pet animal.

Collectively, these stories build a picture of a society incapable of helping itself. We almost never see neighbors, relatives, community organizations, or NGOs in these clips. We can't tell whether they are really absent, or whether their exclusion is just part of the genre.

The press and electronic media are now reflecting the image of a society which is dysfunctional, incapable of getting itself together, and in need of the paternal care which can only be provided by people in positions of authority.

This is the subtle side of authoritarianism. When the government passes an emergency decree which shreds the constitution, people welcome it in part because they have been softened up by a daily drip-feed of bad news.

Lords of the jungle

MYTHS OF THE "GOOD" COUP

2 October 2006

Over the last week, one myth has almost achieved the status of "fact"—that pro-Thaksin forces made the first move on the night of the 19 September. This myth justifies the coup-makers. They were "acting in self-defense." They "had no choice." In some tellings, this sequence even explains why the generals had to rip up the constitution so quickly, because the pro-Thaksin aggression forfeited all constitutional legitimacy.

This myth is not being peddled by the coup-makers themselves. They say they moved because of corruption, disunity, and threats to the monarchy. These are long-term reasons, and straight out of the text book.

Rather, this myth is being peddled by people who are surprised and a little shamefaced to find themselves supporting a coup. This myth makes the coup reactive and defensive. It gives a little salve for some last shreds of democratic conscience. As a senior and irreproachably democratic figure told Chang Noi last week, "I'm sad that I'm not angry."

But there does not seem to be any evidence at all. There were no opposing troops movements on the night of the nineteenth, no reports of armed clashes or even bloodless stand-offs. News that troops were on the move started to spread before 9 p.m. Thaksin appeared on television around ten with a statement that showed he was reacting to a move by his opponents. But by that time, Government House was being surrounded, and Thaksin's point man, General Ruangroj Mahasaranon was switching sides.

General Saprang Kalayanamitr, commander of the Third Army, said last week that the planning began around seven months in advance. That probably means at the time of the Shin Corp sale, when the outburst of anger showed a coup could rely on popular support in the capital. General Sonthi Boonyaratglin's remark about two days' lead time probably means that was when the plan was activated. He has also said on record that the precise moment was chosen because his troops had positional advantage over their opponents. Among the coup-makers there is no recourse to the argument that this was a reactive or pre-emptive strike. It was planned, deliberate, strategic, methodical.

In a slight variant, some have argued that General Sonthi "had to" move because Thaksin was preparing to smash the PAD demonstrations and declare a state of emergency. Chang Noi would welcome evidence to support all these arguments, but there doesn't seem to be a shred.[48]

Who benefits most from this coup? What has changed since April when the king stated that Clause 7 was inappropriate, and urged the judiciary to use methods available under the constitution? Perhaps the answers to these two questions are related. Perhaps too we have to think back to May 1992, and the aftermath of the killings on Ratchadamnoen Avenue. Soldiers were spat upon in the streets, and refused service in shops and hospitals. The army lost face, prestige, budget, secondary forms of employment, opportunities for corruption, and its special privileged role in the state. Ever since, the army has been searching for rehabilitation. It has pushed for a role in development work, drug busting, even tourism. This coup delivers redemption from the catastrophe of 1992. The current craze for "combat chic" may not last, and the military elite will not fully recover its role as the political caste. But they are back at the center of Thai politics—with a vengeance.

But they and their Bangkok supporters are marooned on an island. On one side there is a sea of international opinion, appalled at how the beacon of democracy in Southeast Asia could have bombed itself back into the political stone age. On the other is the rural mass, probably unsurprised but massively resentful at this treatment of the first

---

48. According to this myth, Thaksin planned a bloody crackdown on the Sondhi Limthongkul demonstrations on the following day, and thus the army had to move quickly to prevent death and bloodshed. This makes no sense. By the unwritten laws of Thai politics, if Thaksin had been responsible for death and bloodshed in the center of the capital, his political career would have come to a rapid close. Allowing the crackdown to go ahead would have been a brilliant way to get rid of him.

political leader they had embraced as their own. Why should they ever again listen to city slickers preaching to them about democracy?

A second myth is right there in the coup-makers' first line of self-justification: that this coup will overcome disunity. Reconciliation does not come out of the barrel of a gun. Unity cannot descend from above. The coup-makers themselves are divided; the armed forces are divided; and the country is now divided worse than before. Moreover, things are likely to get worse.

History tells us that no political regime flourishes in Thailand when economic growth falls much below 5 percent. Looking ahead to next year, that figure already seems unattainable. Growth has slackened as a result of world conditions. Investments have been delayed, and will be delayed yet further. Tourism will suffer. Slow growth will mean rising unemployment, and faltering tourism will mean less income for a lot of little people.

Bread can be substituted with circuses, but only over the short term. The political attention span of the Bangkok middle-class is notoriously short. The coup-installed government will try to stave off boredom by revelations of corruption. The Khunying Jaruvarn show[49] will run and run. But the series will only become a hit if the plot has lots of blood and gore. Again history tells us that Thai coup regimes always promise to clean up corruption, but regularly fail. This corruption circus will certainly fail if it does not feature the big star that everybody expects. Any hint of the usual kind of amnesty deal will see the ratings collapse.

The honeymoon will not survive the rows that will erupt over the drafting of a new constitution. This is an area where there are real rifts of ideology. Since the experience with the 1997 charter, more people understand the constitution's importance, and more will want a say. Take the matter of whether the Senate should be appointed or elected (and how, in either case), or whether there should be any Senate at all. This issue has the power to revive ideas and partisanship which are backed by a half-century of history.

---

49. See page 74, note 25.

A conservative shift in the political regime emboldens the more conservative elements in the political culture. The bureaucratic old guard was pushed into the background by Thaksin, and has been curdling resentment for five years. Over just the last week, old-guard health bureaucrats have begun mobilizing to kill the 30-baht scheme by administrative carpet-bombing, and fiscal conservatives are plotting to wipe away all the Thaksin government's social schemes. Such forces are stupid and insensitive enough to ignore the political consequences.

Oh dear.

GIVING UP ON DEMOCRACY

27 November 2006

Over the past few days, Sondhi Limthongkul has made a mini-tour of the US, talking to audiences of Thais and interested observers. His message was stark. The experience of Thaksin has shown that electoral democracy cannot work in Thailand. The mass of rural people who constitute the largest element in the electorate do not have the knowledge to participate properly. They sell their votes, either retail to the local canvasser, or wholesale to the populist who promises them goodies. This commercialism breeds a style of politician who is greedy and corrupt. The last few years have shown that a constitution, however well crafted, cannot impose any semblance of good governance.

What Sondhi says is important because he served as the spark for the Bangkok middle class's emotional rejection of Thaksin. In many ways, he was a surprising candidate for this role. He had been one of Thaksin's most fervent supporters for five years. The two men are very similar. If you set out to clone Thaksin and made a tiny mistake you might finish up creating Sondhi. He became a key leader of the anti-Thaksin movement for two reasons: he had rare access to media outlets, and he changed his own tune to brilliantly articulate Bangkok middle-class opinion. We have to pay attention to him because he is undoubtedly still trying to channel this middle-class voice.

What he is saying is not new, but as old as Thailand's first fragile experiments with democracy. Underlying his views are the city's fear of the countryside, the middle-class fear of the peasant.

In 1932, the pioneers of Thailand's middle-class politicians stopped short of ushering in a new democracy on grounds the provinces were not yet ready. In the 1970s, the middle class backed the military to thwart a pro-peasant insurgency. In the 1990s, the middle class quietly cheered the Democrat governments for turning their backs on rural protesters, and occasionally beating them over the head.

Underlying this fear is the huge divide in Thai society—not just the massive inequality in incomes, but the great imbalance in the distribution of social services and public goods, and also the cultural gap which has widened as the city has grown richer, more confident, and more dazzled by globalization.

Over a decade ago, the political scientist Anek Laothammatas mused on the political consequences of having the society divided into two virtual nations. The city people harbor dreams of a Western-style liberal democracy, but the villagers send gangsters as MPs to the capital to wrestle away whatever resources they can bring back to their constituencies while making some private benefit on the side. The constant clash of these two political cultures results in endemic political instability. Anek's answer was to educate the villagers in democracy, but also to put their needs on the national political agenda so that the gangsters would no longer have a role.

To a very large extent, Thaksin was following that second part of Anek's agenda. The platform his advisers assembled before the 2001 election was simply a collection of measures which the rural electors said they wanted. The claim he made at the 2005 poll was that he alone could act as a channel for rural demands because other parties were not interested.

Thaksin's populism was sometimes crude, often extravagant, and always a cover for corruption, cronyism, and profiteering. But what made this populism truly frightening for the middle class—and hence the focus of Sondhi's tirade—was its political implications. Thaksin was giving political legitimacy to rural demands. If this trend were followed to its logical conclusion, it would undermine the city's undue share of government spending and public goods. There would also be a bill, which the well-off might be asked to pay.

Sondhi is appealing to a deep vein of middle-class fear. Bangkokians no longer have to worry about rural revolution, and have even been spared the sight of rural protesters cluttering up the Bangkok pavements (an unappreciated benefit of the Thaksin era). But they understand that deep down electoral politics is a battle over the command of resources, and that Thaksin's populism showed the rural mass was starting to gain a larger share.

Seven years ago, on the eve of Thaksin's rise, Chang Noi wrote a piece on this same theme, joking that Bangkok would like to copy the Singapore Solution (giving away your rural hinterland, as Singapore did by splitting from Malaysia) or build a Great Wall round the city.[50] But Sondhi's solution is serious. He is turning his back on the last seventy-five years of Thailand's political history, saying that Thailand's social reality makes electoral democracy unworkable and constitutions futile.

Compared to Anek's proposals of a decade earlier, Sondhi's thinking represents a considerable hardening of attitudes. He claims he will continue to work for democracy, but only with the middle class because they alone understand that populist politicians abuse power. By implication, the rural masses do not qualify for this "democracy" so they must be excluded or contained.

This thinking may find its way into the drafting of the new constitution, in the form of measures designed to upweight the effective representation of Bangkok, and downweight that of the countryside (for example, through a Senate partly appointed and partly elected as a single national constituency).

But this will fail. Thaksin became a populist not because he was born a populist but because he recognized there was a political demand which he could exploit to gain and retain power. Thaksin's populism does not show, as Sondhi claims, that the rural electorate is stupid, but rather that it is becoming more politicized and more astute in getting what it wants. Removing Thaksin from the political scene will not destroy the populism he came to represent. A constitutional solution which tries to ensure that rural demands do not get the hearing they deserve in the formal politics of the nation will simply redirect those demands elsewhere.

---

50. See "The Great Wall of Bangkok," pp. 142–44.

DREAMS OF NATIONAL UNITY

22 January 2007

Over the last few weeks, Chang Noi has spent a lot of time traveling in Bangkok taxis. Usually you need some small talk before asking about politics. But the drivers launched off unprompted almost before the door was closed and the meter button pressed. The message went something like this.

"Why did they get rid of him? Everything is getting worse, going slower. People are not spending money like before, instead they're waiting. Projects are all stopped. The stock market is down. Tourists are staying away. It affects us taxis, you know. My daily takings are down, way down.

"It's even worse back in the village. The price of rice has dropped to around half. How can people survive? And the army is making all sorts of trouble. I can't even drive this taxi home and bring my family to Bangkok. I'll get stopped. If you ask me, 99.9 percent of taxi drivers want him back. And 99.9 percent of people in the village want him back."

CN: "But people say he didn't respect the king. You love the king and you want Thaksin back. Why does there seem to be a problem?"

Taxi: "Yes. That puzzles me too (*phom ko ngong mueankan*)."

One of the four reasons that the junta gave for staging the coup was that Thaksin had "caused an unprecedented rift in society" and they "needed to seize power to control the situation, to restore normalcy and to create unity as soon as possible."

Unity is a standard piece of Thai coup rhetoric, and of Thai military ideology. The military began justifying its power on grounds it had the ability to create unity back in the 1930s. The formula became especially important during the Cold War. The word has tended to surface in the self-justification of coups which shut down the democratic process (1947, 1976, 2006). The party concocted by the junta to extend its power after the 1991 coup was called Samakkhitham, the party of righteous unity.

But unity does not mean what it claims to mean. No society is truly unified. What unity means is acceptance, tolerance, resignation, or perhaps, simplest of all, defeat. After 1976, the military imposed unity by crushing popular organizations, hiring vigilante groups in the villages, intimidating local leaders, and disappearing those who did not get the message. The result was not unity, but sullen acceptance.

The divisions that disunite Thai society are very real. They have got worse over the last generation as the economy rode a rollercoaster of boom and bust, the tycoons made fortunes way beyond the dreams of earlier years, the urban middle class became wrapped up in globalization and turned its back on its own society, and the rural economy fell steadily further and further behind.

The politicization of this division was inevitable, but developed rather slowly. By the late 1980s, the Cold War was over, insurgency was dead, and the military stopped policing the politics of the mass. Through the 1990s, NGOs and local movements galvanized people around issues of rights, livelihood, resources, and environment. In 1997, villagers were hit by a massive crisis which they had done nothing to cause, which caused them untold grief, and for which they got no relief like the financiers and speculators.

Thaksin did not create the disunity. It was there already. Nor did he spark the politicization of that disunity. That had already begun. He simply sharpened it, and profited from it. Removing him does not close the divisions in society by one centimeter.

What has the post-coup government been doing "to restore normalcy and to create unity as soon as possible"? It has taken the subsidy away from rice and thereby brought the price crashing down. It has told the poor, wait, please, we'll get round to you sometime. It has sent a contingent of over thirteen thousand troops to police political activity, so people have a regular reminder of the bad old days a quarter of a century ago. It wants to bring back hopeless and hated projects like the Kaeng Sua Ten dam. It is restricting people moving around. Now the harvest is over, tens of thousands of people leave their home village to find work elsewhere. Whole villages are contracted to go by the truck-load to cut sugarcane in Kanchanaburi, Ratchaburi, and Chon Buri. Now they have to get a permit from local officials, and tolerate hold-ups at countless checkpoints. It's like crossing national boundaries, not moving across your own unified country.

The military doesn't really have any idea how to "create unity." It just knows that in the past it was successful in creating the sullen acceptance that gave a semblance of unity. But the society is not the same as thirty years ago. The rise of elective politics has been truly empowering. The military cannot intimidate as easily as it could in the past. One of the most significant developments since 19 September has been that the party politicians and local politicians have not meekly accepted the coup. They have been openly defiant, regularly calling for the return of parliament.

In a society as complex as modern Thailand, representative institutions, however flawed, are a much better way of managing the divisions and competing interests than authoritarianism wielding a myth of unity. Only people who live outside normal society, in something like the structured world of the military, can dream of unity.

The fear is that as the coup government's policies fail, and their support dwindles, their natural instinct will be do more of what they know best. Already that downward spiral has begun: the retention of martial law, the establishment of the special forces, restrictions on the media, and the order to airbrush Thaksin out of the media in the manner of a totalitarian state.

Perhaps the coup government will eventually achieve unity—by uniting the country against itself.

AGAINST THE COUP

5 March 2007

Many urban people welcomed the 19 September coup. As the six-month anniversary approaches, more and more are having second thoughts. The government is stuttering, news from the charter drafters is depressing, southern violence gets worse, and Thailand's stock in the world sinks ever lower. On current trend, it's not long before Surayud Chulanont's falling ratings meet Thaksin's rising ones. Some blame this on Surayud personally. But others are asking the bigger questions. Why didn't the coup work? Was it a good idea to have a coup in the first place? And if not, why did it happen?

Last month, the magazine *Fa Dieo Kan* (Same Sky) put out a special issue on the coup. The editor apologizes upfront for making no pretence of even balance. This book is unremittingly and furiously against the coup. The contents include articles, speeches, interviews, and translations by twenty people, so there is no single argument, and much disagreement. But the book's overall message is daring, revealing, and very challenging.

The cover tells it all. The graphic lampoons the generals' protests that it was not really a coup. The title is: "The Coup for Democracy with the King as Head of State." The book's first main point is that you cannot start to understand this coup, or current Thai politics at all, without confronting the role of the monarchical institution.

In these writers' usage, the monarchical institution is not an individual or family but a much larger collection of people including privy councilors and royalist supporters. This monarchical institution is like a "black box" in economic or scientific theory. You cannot see inside so you don't know how it works. But you can see what it does and what the effects are on the outside world. Several of the writers argue that the major role of the black box in this coup is undeniable. You need only consider the role of privy councilors both before and after. These writers then ask: why did this happen, and what are the consequences?

Thongchai Winichakul answers these questions using a long perspective. The history of modern Thailand has tended to be written as good democrats combating bad soldiers. But the crucial battle of that war was fought in 1973, and the war ended by 1992. Instead Thongchai suggests the whole dreary history of coups from 1947 onwards should be seen as an attempt by self-serving elites to control the consequences of what happened in 1932. Their goal is not to return to monarchic rule, but to a form of elite rule which clings to the monarchy for legitimacy. But over time the politicians and the people have become pushier. One counter strategy of the old elites is to go on and on about corruption and money politics. In itself, this criticism is not bad. But it can easily become a tool to discredit parliamentary politics as a whole, and overthrow the fundamental concept of democracy—the sovereignty of the people. In Thongchai's words, "If a government supported by a popular majority is only a 'jockey,' then in the end the government machinery belongs to the king."[51]

But how do such historical forces work in practice, in the present? After the coup, General Sonthi Boonyaratglin said he moved at "the

---

51. On 14 July 2006 at the Chulachomklao Royal Military Academy, General Prem said, "soldiers belong to His Majesty the King, not to a government. A government is like a jockey. It supervises soldiers, but the real owners are the country, and the King" (*Bangkok Post*, 15 July 2006). Prem repeated the image in an interview with *Far Eastern Economic Review* shortly before the coup.

request of the people." General Saprang Kalyanamitr let slip that the planning took seven months, meaning it started in February 2006, amid the furor over the Shin Corp sale. Thanapol Eawsakul tracks back to that month to examine the genesis of the coup in fine detail.

Sondhi Limthongkul had begun his crusade several months before—wrapping himself in yellow, splashing "we will fight for the king" across his chest, and claiming to light a "dhamma candle" to spotlight Thaksin's evil. Sondhi created the idea that politics had become a contest between the prime minister and the king. But in late 2005 his movement was stumbling. The rallies were dwindling and Sondhi's allegations of corruption were embarrassingly thin. The Shin Corp sale gave him a second chance.

A week later one of his future PAD allies, Somkiat Phongpaiboon wrote, "Please watch the royalist group and the privy councilors, which Sondhi has called 'the return of the royal power.'"

On 4 February 2006, Thaksin said he would resign if the king whispered in his ear. That evening, Sondhi thundered from his rally stage "Where is the army? This talk is enough to bring [Thaksin] to the execution post." That night he took a petition to General Prem. As he told the world on the following day, the Bureau of the Royal Household was surprisingly open at 9 p.m. as if ready to receive him. Sondhi also went to meet General Sonthi Boonyaratglin, and related later, "I asked [Sonthi], 'Are you going to stand by the people?' He nodded, 'I will stand by the people because I am a soldier of the king.'"

From that point, Sondhi organized more rallies, but they did not build. He called for the use of Clause 7, but on 25 April the king said that would be inappropriate. As Thanapol concludes, the coup happened because Sondhi L. issued an invitation to the army to carry out the coup, and Sonthi B. accepted the invitation.

Given these events, how can monarchy and democracy coexist for the long term, without regular crises? To help answer this question, Sulak Sivaraksa surveys monarchies which survive and prosper in other democratic countries. He concludes there are four conditions: the monarchy "has nothing to do with the generals"; its finances are transparent;

it is seen as working for the people rather than for itself; and it truly supports a democratic form of government.

More people have begun to doubt that this coup was ever the solution to anything. This special issue of *Fa Dieo Kan* argues that the big issue now is not the military or political corruption or populism, but how to prevent an elite minority from controlling politics and keeping the mass as passive partners, in part by exploiting the symbolic power of the monarchy.

THAILAND'S LOST DECADE

14 May 2007

The great themes of Thailand in the 1990s were reform, openness, and participation. Political institutions were overhauled by the most dramatic constitutional reform since 1932. The press was celebrated as among the most free and feisty in Asia. Even electronic media began to ease free of state control. The bureaucracy was at last obliged to distribute power to elective local government. Civil society expanded in an upsurge of organization, protest, and debate. Economic planning was reoriented from growth to social goals. Reforms in education and health care were plotted by private initiative and forced upon a reluctant officialdom.

The great themes of the 2000s have been authoritarianism, suppression, and exclusion. Thaksin Shinawatra used power won at the ballot box to suppress debate, emasculate institutions, favor cronies, and move towards a one-party, one-man state. Electronic media were brought back under close control, print media intimidated, and wars waged against community radio and websites. Thaksin was overthrown by an old-fashioned tank-trundling coup—a maneuver which had last succeeded half a century earlier. Politics are again dominated by individuals and types previously seen under military dictatorship. Political activity is tightly controlled. Media are stifled by intimidation and self-censorship. In a throwback to the old era, rumor has again became a key part of day-to-day politics. The junta hand-picked people to redraft a constitution which reduces the significance of elections, and which places great powers in the hands of a small number of people.

What happened? Why have the dominant trends of these two decades been so contrasting?

Some blame it all on Thaksin for aiming at such a monopoly of power and profit that it provoked such a primitive reaction. Some blame the drafters of the 1997 Constitution for trying to create stronger and more stable governments without imagining how this design could be perverted by massive wealth. Some blame the 1997 economic crisis for undermining the old political order, and shocking Thaksin and his business cronies into making their grab for power.

But stand back a bit and take a broader, longer perspective.

Thailand is grappling with the consequences of the great boom and the great bust. In the great boom, average incomes tripled in a little over a single decade. Across the spectrum of society, people had more wealth, more assets to protect, more interests to promote. At the top, new fortunes were created at a speed and on a scale never previously experienced. In short, the social order changed irrevocably.

Then the great bust delivered a staggering shock. An economy which had grown unfailingly for four decades suddenly shrank more than anyone thought possible. Businesses were bankrupted, millions unemployed, thousands forced back below the poverty line. The great bust impelled more people into politics, often to defend what they had gained over the great boom. They flocked to street demonstrations, supported new parties, and participated in intense debate over Thailand's future.

Politics will only become stable when the political system reflects and accommodates the new social order, economic interests, and political aspirations which have been created in these extraordinary two decades.

But the leadership since the late 1990s has totally failed to confront this challenge.

The Democrats who came to power in 1997 refused to accept the new order. They would not listen to the new businessmen who complained the government sided too compliantly with the IMF. They looked the other way when farmers took to the streets to complain they were left to bear the brunt of the crisis. As a result, the party was annihilated in the 2001 elections.

Thaksin Shinawatra emerged as the leader of exactly those political forces which the Democrats ignored. He articulated the ambitions of the new generation of businessmen made wealthy by the great boom. Perhaps despite himself, he also turned into a populist and built a bridge between the new mass politics and the parliamentary system. But he failed to acknowledge that the old order still had interests to protect, and influence to do so. He provoked the elite. He stirred up the army. He antagonized the bureaucrats. He made the urban middle class fear that they would become politically irrelevant, and would pay the bill for enriching Thaksin's clique and buying him mass support.

The junta has taken this politics of exclusion to another extreme by banning all political activity, and bringing back old-fashioned government by bureaucrats. Policymaking is not responsive to the major interests in the country, but to minority lobbies of economic nationalists, cultural atavists, and moral crusaders who have access to these dinosaurs.

For the longer term the junta hopes to impose a constitution which excludes the social and political forces they don't know how to control. The draft charter is an attempt to limit the importance of elections in determining who has power, while institutionalizing a cozy little elite from the celestial ranks of the military, bureaucracy, and judiciary.

This won't work. A political system is a set of rules and institutions for managing the various and conflicting demands on the state. Such systems work well when enough of the important interests accept that this set of rules is fair and workable. Otherwise there are powerful groups which feel forced to play outside the rules, and which tear up the rule book at the slightest opportunity.

The process for drawing up such a set of rules has to be inclusive. A hand-picked group of old school friends working within a deliberately restrictive framework cannot possibly succeed. Probably it will be best if this constitution-making process fails, either in the Drafting Assembly or the referendum.

That will create the opportunity to begin a more inclusive process which has some chance of creating a workable set of rules. But an acceptable constitution is only part of the problem. Key political forces have to be persuaded to work within a set of rules, however uncomfortable, rather than resorting to force and high-handedness. The dismal failure of this coup-installed government should serve as education. Or is that too hopeful?

A STATE AT WAR WITH ITS PEOPLE

9 September 2007

The Internal Security Act which the junta wants to pass is the key measure to reinstate the army high command at the peak of the government.

On first appearance, the law seems to set up a new organization, or at least revive an old one—the Internal Security Operations Command, ISOC, which was originally formed to combat communism and had faded into the background in recent years. But this is an illusion. What the law does is give massive new powers to the army chief. In the past, the directorship of ISOC was a stand-alone post with its own secretariat and organization. In this law, the army chief automatically becomes head of ISOC. The chief of the army general staff heads up the ISOC secretariat. The regional army chiefs become the ISOC regional heads. The whole point of the bill is to give more powers to the army and especially the army chief.

And these powers are considerable. Arrest. Detention. Search. Curfew. Confinement to a house. Blocking roads. Seizing and confiscating anything. Banning meetings, gatherings, entertainment, and publicity. Demanding documents and other evidence. In most cases, no warrants or authorization are required. Even when they are, these can be dispensed with "in case of emergency." Under one extraordinary clause, an authorized official can tell anybody to do anything. This act creates a pervasive and permanent state of semi-martial law.

These powers can supposedly be invoked only to prevent or resolve threats to internal security. But the definition of internal security is very broad. It includes violent acts, but also "propaganda" or "publicity." We know from experience that those in power tend to portray any opposition to themselves as threats to national security. A year ago Thaksin was making claims of that nature. Only a few months later some soldiers growled that remarks about Sonthi Boonyaratglin's marital circumstances or Surayud Chulanont's holiday accommodation were threats to national security.

In the bill draft, there is no real monitor or check on the use of this wide-ranging authority. The army head exercises these powers in his own right, not as the agent of the prime minister. The act specifies that he reports directly to the prime minister but there is no mechanism provided for the prime minister or cabinet to exercise any oversight. The act sets up committees to oversee ISOC at the national, regional, and provincial level, but these committees are largely appointed by the army.

In short, this act gives very considerable powers to the army chief. It makes him in many ways more powerful than the prime minister, and not really answerable to anyone. A state above the state.

To understand this legislation, it helps to know the background. The army began campaigning for this law in February 1998 when the Chuan government announced it would repeal the tired old Anti-Communist Act of 1952 (the repeal was completed in June 2001). The army argued that it would need a new legal basis to operate after this old act lapsed. This is very telling. For what exactly did the army need a new legal basis to operate?

The Anti-Communist Act was passed in a context of war—the so-called Cold War which outside the rich countries was not "cold" at all. In that era, the army and the rebels saw one another as enemies, and fought pitched battles. All today's top brass (Sonthi, Surayud, Vinai, Saprang, Anupong) took part in this conflict during the formative period of their lives. This new draft security law is a direct descendent of the Anti-Communist Act. It is littered with some of the characteristic vocabulary of the Cold War era. It talks about unity (*samakkhi*), peace and order (*khwam sangop riaproi*), uniting the power of the masses, and protecting nation, religion, and king. The mindset is very clear.

The new Act is not needed to deal with the far south. The State of Emergency Decree passed in 2005 was designed for that and is still being used for that purpose. That emergency decree could also be used against terrorism or drug trafficking. The whole point about this Act is that it is always in force and everywhere in force, pervasive and permanent.

There is another telling sign. The draft of the bill is very sloppy. The language is inconsistent. Typos abound. Several sections are a big muddle. One amazing clause appears to require anyone thinking of starting an illegal business to keep proper personnel records. The draft has all the signs of being a hasty cut-and-paste job from old sources. Several clauses have been scissored out of the State of Emergency Decree introduced two years ago. In short, it looks like a back-of-the-envelope job by one of the junta's legal hitmen.

This makes one speculate why the junta recently added sixty days to its potential time in power. This extra time is not really needed to complete all the legislation for a new election. Correcting the old organic laws should consume a long afternoon at most. No, one suspects that the junta needs extra time to pass this internal security law and maybe some others.

And what does that tell us? That the junta knows it's at war. That having martyred a popular political leader and martyred a popular political party, it may now be facing a considerable enemy. That the army cannot afford to "restore democracy" the way it wants without equipping itself with very impressive powers to use against internal enemies.

Last September, the coup-makers talked a lot about reconciliation. Probably they got the word wrong. They must have meant capitulation, surrender.[52]

---

52. The Act was passed into law by parliament on 20 December 2007, three days before the general election. The Council of State had amended the draft, making the prime minister head of ISOC and the army chief his deputy, introducing a monitoring committee, and removing some of the provisions providing immunity. But the Act as passed still allowed a very wide interpretation of internal security and provided very considerable powers to the army.

THE NEW COLD WAR

26 November 2007

The army seems to have its own view of the current situation in the country, and has defined for itself a prominent role in confronting this situation. This conclusion comes from various documents which are floating around, and whose authenticity has not been denied.[53] It is confirmed by recent actions and policies which are consistent with this way of thinking.

The army's analysis of the current situation goes like this. There is a "war for the people" in process, meaning a contest for popular support. On one side is the army. On the other are politicians, and especially former communist activists who lurk in the background of party politics. A generation ago, the army won the Cold War in Thailand by dragging the communist rebels back from the jungle to a normal life in the city. But, this analysis contends, the activists have never changed their way of thinking or forsaken their ambitions. They aim to use popular support to grab state power, and then to use state power to implement their own agenda, which includes overthrow of the monarchy. Although the activists now seek popular support through the ballot box, this is not significantly different from the old guerilla strategy of mobilizing the villages. Their tools now are the populist policies offered to the electorate. These policies are designed solely to win popular support and gain election to political office. They do not truly solve the problems of the people. Unless something is done to halt this trend, the army analysis concludes, Thailand will find itself in the same situation as

---

53. This piece summarizes a leaked document from the army Planning Department dated 26 September 2007 and signed by Sonthi Boonyaratglin as army chief. The document contains transcripts of two speeches given to a meeting of army brass on 21 September, and a summary of their content for action plans. The document was leaked through a pro-Thaksin website. Its authenticity was never denied.

Nepal where Maoists have built massive popular support and are trying to replace the monarchy.

According to this view, the army has no larger duty at present than fighting this new Cold War. Threats to the country from the outside are insignificant, except for the intrusion of drugs and illegal immigrants. Even the situation in the far south is judged less serious. But the army seems to be already on the defensive in this "war for the people." It feels it must "win back" the people, especially at the grassroots.

From this analysis of the situation flow strategies and action plans. Several recent actions seem quite consistent with these plans.

First, to win the "war for the people," the army must be an exemplary institution which is worthy of the respect and support of the people. Certainly, in recent months the media have carried few or no stories about soldiers engaged in protection rackets, drug dealing, or other misdemeanors. Army radio is currently broadcasting a line which goes like this: the Thai army is unique amongst the militaries of the world in that it works for the people and is responsible in large part for the country's successful development; this fact has gained acknowledgment all over the world.

Second, the army must gain the support of other official agencies as allies in this war for the people. Under the conditions created by the coup, army men have had the opportunity to insert themselves into the workings of government at all levels. The army must use this position to persuade officials to embrace the view of the current situation outlined above, and to accept the implications for action.

Third, ministries and other bureaucratic agencies must draw up long-terms plans and insist upon following these plans in their day-to-day operations so that politicians who are put in charge of these agencies will not be able to implement the policies they promise to the electorate.

Fourth, as a first stage of regaining popular support, the army must concentrate on merchants, businessmen, and the middle classes. Programs with this target have already been launched.

Fifth, the Internal Security Operations Command (ISOC) units at the regional and the provincial level must play the key role in mobilizing people at the grassroots to support the army. These ISOC units can use the *kamnan*, village headmen, and other official bodies at the local level as their tools to win the "war for the people." The recent changes, which have converted the *kamnan* and village headmen back from elective to bureaucratic positions, are consistent with this strategy. Ideally the provincial ISOC units should take control of issues like drugs, illegal migration, terrorism, poverty eradication, and drought and flood relief so that these policies are more efficient and help win popular support. To ensure success, army officers need to be better educated and more politically aware so that they are more effective leaders. Demobbed soldiers should be organized to supplement the serving troops, because the military budget is still insufficient.

Sixth, if these plans are made known to the public, there is a risk that the army will be accused of digging up the past and reviving dictatorship. Hence, these plans must be implemented using a softly-softly approach, winning the support of strategic allies at every point.

The implications of this army strategy are very deep and wide ranging. Here only a couple of points can be made.

The urgency to pass the Internal Security Act is clearly linked to this "war for the people," and especially to the aim of using provincial ISOC units to fight this war at the grassroots. The legislators supporting the bill should be aware of this.

These plans were drafted when it still looked possible for the army to engineer a tame coalition through the ballot box on 23 December. As this seems less and less likely, what must the army do to implement this strategy?

Although the military budget has increased by over 50 percent in the last fifteen months, largely at the expense of social and economic projects, the army hopes for more funds to pursue this strategy.

The fact these plans have floated into the public domain suggests the army is far from united behind them.

How can such a blinkered, outdated, fear-ridden, divisive, authoritarian, manipulative approach ever lead in the direction of democracy?

POLITICS AND THE STARS

11 December 2007

At a shrine in Chiang Mai in the middle of last month, two generals from the junta and the wife of a third sat under a three-legged arch decorated with banana plants, sugarcane, coconut fronds, bunches of bananas, gourds, candles, incense sticks, and offerings of food. A sacred thread was strung from the peak of the arch around the heads of the three participants who sat with clasped hands while learned monks from sixteen *wat* in the city chanted for two hours.

According to reports of this secret ceremony, the participants were Air Chief Marshal Chalit Phukphasuk, Admiral Sathiraphan Keyanon, and Sasini, wife of General Winai Phattiyakul. The army chief, General Anupong Paochinda, was reluctant to attend in person but sent the deputy chief of the First Army as his representative. The group flew to Chiang Mai in a special plane. The junta members, including General Sonthi Boonyaratglin, had made a group visit to the same shrine in April. Sonthi did not attend this time because it was already too late to improve his fortune.

The rite was reportedly staged because the planetary disposition of the junta has entered a difficult phase, resulting in the decline of the junta's political fortunes which is readily apparent to everyone. General Sonthi's personal horoscope is especially vexed, and on top he has come under attack using the dark arts. An image of the general has been made according to a magical formula, and then subjected to maltreatment in order to cause harm. Sonthi's decision to withdraw himself from the upcoming election, after earlier showing his clear intention of running, is reportedly linked with these events.

The rite was arranged by Varin Buaviratlert who has become Thailand's most famous astrologer. In fact his services range much more widely than prediction based on the movement of heavenly bodies and other signals. He is a spirit medium who channels the spirit of a powerful ascetic named Kewalan who resides in the Himalaya mountains. The site of last month's rite is named the Hall of the Reverend Rishi Kewalan. The generals' secret ceremony was held in the VIP room on the edges of an annual event organized for people who wish to improve their fortune.

Varin rose to national fame by predicting the 16 September 2006 coup. But he has long had a reputation for his powers, especially among the men in green. General Sonthi had earlier consulted him over his career prospects. Varin discovered that Sonthi had been a general of King Taksin (r. 1767–1782) in a past life and was destined to save the country. He predicted Sonthi's somewhat unexpected rise to become army commander, and helped him with rituals to clinch the prediction. Now Varin is so famous and important that he is guarded by Special Forces troops, his visitors are subject to inspection, and his movements are kept secret.

Varin advises his clients on methods to "correct karma" or "sustain fortune." Mostly this requires the client to visit many Buddhist *wat*, listen to chanting, and make donations of money, robes, and other articles. Countering the attack on Sonthi through maltreatment of a magical image might have required something more serious. Usually it is necessary to find and destroy the image, or participate in some rather exacting ceremonial.

At his recent sessions, Varin apparently reported Kewalan's predictions on the near future. For the generals who feel beset by misfortune, these predictions were comforting. Another coup may be in the offing. There is a possibility of a national government. Although the details and timing are far from clear, the political future seems smothered in green. The medium tried to concentrate on Abhisit but the image would not stabilize, and in a flash was overlaid by men in uniform.

Thai politics have long been at the mercy of spirits, stars, and dark forces. As Chavalit Yongchaiyudh's political fortunes collapsed in the 1997 crisis, an adept advised his wife never to go anywhere without a toy elephant. Could it have been coincidence that the fortunes of the Democrat Party dived in 2000-1 after disaster befell the party's trademark statue of the earth goddess, Mae Thorani? The 2006 coup occurred shortly after the Brahma image at the Erawan junction had been destroyed. For many years no politician could hope for success in the northeast until he had been bashed on the head with a roll of paper by the country's most famous "magic monk," Luang Por Koon. The King Prajadhipok Institute, established to upgrade the quality of Thai politics, hosted a seminar for political astrologers earlier this year.

Although presenting himself as a politician for the new age of modernity, Thaksin took trouble to get the spirits and stars on his side. He patronized a northeastern monk who specialized in predicting election results until the monk's life was complicated by a criminal charge. In advance of the crucial court verdict on his asset-concealment case, Thaksin sponsored prayer chanting in several *wat*. When opposition against him swelled in 2004, he made several visits to a famous seer named ET in Rangoon. In the endgame prior to the coup, Newin Chidchob arranged for Thaksin to benefit from Khmer rites and practices in southern Isan, including walking under an elephant.

Although Varin is now closely associated with the junta, Thaksin and Pojaman also count among his fans. Reportedly last month Pojaman paid him a visit for advice on how to "correct her karma" and improve her husband's chances of returning home. Varin prescribed some *wat* visits and donations.

Whether politicians are hi-tech businessmen with billions at their fingertips, or generals with battlefield experience and command over thousands of men, they are reluctant to feel that their political careers depend on the will of the people. They prefer to put their faith in planetary movements, spirits, dark forces, chanting, offerings, Burmese seers, Khmer magic, and dead Himalayan ascetics.

BULLDOG ON A LEASH OR ANOTHER
NAIL IN DEMOCRACY'S COFFIN?

21 July 2008

Since it was formed in February 2006, and especially since it was revived in May this year, the People's Alliance for Democracy, has become a very distinctive force in the political landscape. Formally, PAD is simply an alliance of five orators. But as a political phenomenon, PAD is also what they are saying, how they are saying it, what visual messages they convey, and who is supporting them.

The movement's main stated aim is to overthrow the current government. Normally any movement which professed this aim would be labeled dangerous, even revolutionary, and be strongly handled by the authorities. Strangely that is not happening. Probably that is because we know its true aim is to obstruct Thaksin's overt return to politics.

The movement's longer-term aim is to undermine the central principles of electoral democracy, namely the sovereignty of the people, and the selection of a parliament by the system of one-man, one-vote. The PAD leaders claim that the electorate cannot be trusted with the franchise because the mass of rural people are uneducated and corrupt. They want the elected portion of the lower house reduced to a minority (perhaps 30 percent), and the remainder filled partly by "retired officials and important people" and partly by ordinary people and workers, selected by appointment. Since the logic of the PAD's proposal is to disenfranchise the rural poor, this new system is likely to favor the rich, the urban, and the higher educated.

In addition, PAD wants the military to have a permanent role of political oversight. The military would be removed from political control (by making the Defense Ministry independent of the cabinet), and granted a right to intervene in politics to check corruption and to protect the monarchy and national sovereignty.

The PAD seems against the freedom of expression, and in favor of the use of abuse and intimidation to limit the freedom of expression. This conclusion is based on the way that PAD orators treat academics, actors, or other public figures that have disagreed with PAD views. This tactic seems to have been quite successful. Some critics have apologized. The press has been generally rather uncritical of the PAD's views and activities.

The PAD makes use of military and martial symbolism. Some of the leaders like to wear brown shirts and black shirts that resemble military and para-military uniforms. The headbands worn by leaders and followers recall the outfits of traditional warriors, samurai, and jungle fighters. The oversized neckscarf comes from the scouts, village scouts, and jungle fighters. It is not Chamlong's rural-ascetic look but this barracks-chic that distinguishes the movement. Among the supporters, yellow flags, headbands, T-shirts, and caps combine to give the impression of commonality and conformity which is the role of uniforms.

PAD promotes a visceral nationalism reminiscent of the early Phibun era. The nation is a body that is being physically ripped by its enemies (internal and external), causing pain to the citizens, who must rise up in the nation's defense.

The PAD's agitational practice suggests a high degree of organization, strong financing, access to technology, and skill with sophisticated techniques. The equipment for staging and broadcasting the PAD's message requires high capital cost and running expenses. The crowds are well organized and provisioned. The programming shows strategic planning to sustain support and interest with relatively little novelty. The PAD seems skilled in the techniques and rituals of litigation. In short, this is not a few people gathered at a street corner with a soap box.

Analyzing the PAD's audience on the streets and in front of television screens is difficult. There are only stray interviews, plus pictures. Perhaps the single word that emerges from this impressionistic data is "respectable." The crowds are generally smartly dressed. The age-profile is quite high, though there are also many families in attendance (and the TV audience may be significantly younger). Head-counting from press photos shows a slight preponderance of women over men. From the few on-site interviews available, the crowds include retirees, public servants, small business people, and senior executives from modern firms. There seem to be relatively few manual workers.

The PAD is clearly well-connected to other institutions. One of its leaders is a Democrat MP. Other Democrats have spoken from its stages. So too have academics from some of Bangkok's major universities. A serving general has taken the PAD stage in his full uniform. Other military figures, including General Saprang Kalyanamitr, have been seen backstage and are open in their support.

The PAD seems to be protected, perhaps by friends in important places, but also by virtue of its widespread urban support. No other Bangkok protest has suffered so little harassment. When the prime minister angrily threatened to clear PAD off the streets, the security forces refused to cooperate and the prime minister had to back down. When PAD set up a permanent blockade of roads, the police stood aside and public-opinion surveys were surprisingly lenient over the disruption to traffic. When the protest moved to Government House, the police resistance looked like a token showing designed to fail. This apparent immunity gives weight to PAD's message.

The PAD is flirting with the old agent provocateur's technique of placing its own crudely armed gangs in places where they will be attacked by enemies. This creates violent incidents, apparently initiated by their opponents, though in truth a result of the inherent violence of the PAD itself.

In short, PAD is an anti-democratic movement, supported by high investment and shadowy protection, that exploits the fears of the privileged and a deliberately anti-rational nationalism, and flirts with militarism and violence.

Is PAD a bulldog, let out on a leash for a specific purpose, that will be chained up when the threat from thieves has passed? Or is it another step in the destruction of democracy begun by Thaksin, continued by the coup-makers, and now plunging ahead on the momentum?

Tail piece

THE GREAT BANGKOK NOVEL

16 May 2001

Lately there has been a fad for novels set in Thailand. It looks easy. Chang Noi is thinking of writing one, too. Here's the outline of chapter one.

The scene opens on a Bangkok street. A pickup has stalled. A policeman goes to investigate. The driver seems nervous, so the policeman looks inside the truck. To his surprise, he finds a bundle of money. Within a couple of pages, the police have raided the driver's apartment and found more bundles. Millions and millions of baht. They realize they have stumbled on the money-laundering operation for the cross-border drug trade.

We switch to a newspaper newsroom. The crime journalist has talked to his police contacts and acquired the list of companies found in the money launderers' apartment. He slips into his computer a CD with the registration details of all Thai companies, and starts to search. The first company is managed by the wife of the former commander of the army unit which guards the border where the drugs come across. The boards of other companies on the list are stuffed with other officers from this army. Names of other important people appear. Then—bingo!—the speaker of the Senate. The journalist reaches for the phone.

We switch to an office in the Senate. The speaker is a blocky man who moves stiffly like a robot needing oil. He is talking into the phone. Yes, he is acquainted with the army commander. No, he did not know he was a director of the named company. He puts down the phone. His face is bathed in a light sweat. But not because of this phone call. This new problem is a fleabite compared to his other troubles. The Election Commission is threatening to cancel his Senate seat for electoral malpractice. His deputy has just been accused of sex with under-age schoolgirls. One of his advisers is being accused of soliciting millions of baht in bribes from candidates for a commission that will control the telecommunications industry. Some say this adviser had faked his educational qualifications and changed his own name thirty-four times.

On a TV screen in the corner of the room, this adviser is being interviewed about his relationship with the Senate speaker: "I was just like a flower to him. He picked me, adored me for a while and finally threw me away. There are many interesting stories I will tell next week. I'm the type who likes collecting dirt. I will have an eye for an eye." The telephone rings. It is another journalist asking about the speaker and his adviser. The speaker replies, "Yes, he was my adviser. But I never asked him for any advice."

The office door opens. The man who enters has a military bearing. He looks like a cross between Peter Cushing and Hannibal Lector. Although he is only an ordinary senator, he seems to treat the speaker like a subordinate. He is not sympathetic to the speaker's troubles because he has worries of his own.

A dead governor has been found in a downtown hotel. Now, governors are like gods. They are very, very rarely found murdered. They are never found brutally shot and stabbed in a hotel room. Moreover, the room opposite was booked in the name of one of Hannibal's former military aides. The governor's blood is all over this room and the aide's car. According to reports, the aide and his friends arrived at the hotel after a gambling session, and ordered up some girls from room service. The aide has already come under criminal suspicion three times for murder, for running a protection racket, and for setting fire to a shopping mall. Hannibal was implicated in the protection case, but somehow all the charges failed "for lack of evidence." Hannibal's brother was recently picked up on suspicion of trading arms near the border. Some people have called Hannibal a "dark influence." Times are bad.

We go back to the newsroom. For the next few pages, the novel follows the paper's crime reporter. The police have picked up a young woman. She was the governor's girlfriend. By some accounts, she was also the military aide's girlfriend. Under interrogation, she confesses to murdering the governor. She says it was the only way she could think of ending the affair. But the police are doubtful. They can think of other ways to end an affair. They don't believe such a slight female could inflict such a brutal murder on such a big man. Plus there's the blood all over the car and the other room. They interrogate her again. Now she denies it. But she does admit she was present. That means she must know who did it. The police seem surprisingly reluctant to talk to Hannibal's military aide. Instead, they summon the girlfriend again. In the middle of questioning, she slips out to the toilet in the police station, leaves a note with a confession, and tries to hang herself.

Whew! How are we doing? We haven't got to the end of chapter one and already we have drugs, murder, money-laundering, bribery, gun-running, corruption, protection rackets, pedophilia, blackmail, arson, and attempted suicide. What are we going to do for a climax? What shall we call it? What about "The Senate"? It has a good Grishamesque ring. But it's already been used.

On reflection, all these recent novels are set in Thailand, but they are not really *about* Thailand. You can see why. Any novel about Thailand would have to compete with reality.[54]

---

54. Apart from the journalist invented as a linking device, all of the events including the quotations were taken directly from news reports in the few weeks before this piece was written. The speaker of the Senate, Sanit Worapanya, was found to be shareholder in a company linked to the United Wa Army. Weeks later he was ejected from the Senate for poll fraud. He stood for reelection but lost, and appealed against the ejection but lost. His deputy, Chalerm Promlert, was charged for having sex in a motel with five under-age schoolgirls. He was sentenced to sixteen years, increased to thirty-six by the Supreme Court after he appealed. The adviser, Aphiphon Kongchanakun, was charged with bribery over the selection of members of the National Telecommunication Commission, but the case disappeared. "Hannibal" is Major-General Intharat Yodbangtoey, known as Se Moi. The governor of Yasothon Province murdered in March 2001 was Preena Lipattanaphan. In 2002, Major Charlermchai Matchaklam, an aide to Intharat, was sentenced to death for the murder. His car and shoes had traces of Preena's blood, and a sketch of the hotel room was found in his possession. The girl, Ankhanang Sunthornwiphak, told the court she was lying face down on a couch when Preena was shot. She was sentenced to three years eight months in jail for pawning Preena's ring. In 2006, the Supreme Court upheld the death sentence for Chalermchai and two soldier accomplices. The motive for Chalermchai committing the murder was never addressed or explained. The police reckoned he was a paid killer. Major-General Intharat is now deputy leader of the Matchima Thippatai Party. The links between the speaker, generals, and Wa-linked companies were never investigated.